# A Stranger Within

## Paulette Riddlesprigger

WestBow
PRESS
A DIVISION OF THOMAS NELSON

**NIV—New International Version**
Scriptures taken from the Holy Bible, New International Version®, NIV®. Copyright © 1973, 1978, 1984, 2011 by Biblica, Inc.™ Used by permission of Zondervan. All rights reserved worldwide. www.zondervan.com The "NIV" and "New International Version" are trademarks registered in the United States Patent and Trademark Office by Biblica, Inc.™

**Amplified Bible**
Scripture taken from the *Amplified Bible*, Copyright © 1954, 1958, 1962, 1964, 1965, 1987 by The Lockman Foundation. Used by permission.

**KJV—King James Version**
Scripture taken from the King James Version of the Bible.

**NLT—New Living Translation**
Scripture quotations taken from the Holy Bible, New Living Translation, copyright 1996, 2004. Used by permission of Tyndale House Publishers, Inc., Wheaton, Illinois 60189. All rights reserved.

**The Message Bible**
All Scripture quotations in this publications are from **The Message**. Copyright (c) by Eugene H. Peterson 1993, 1994, 1995, 1996, 2000, 2001, 2002. Used by permission of NavPress Publishing Group.

WestBow Press books may be ordered through booksellers or by contacting:
WestBow Press
A Division of Thomas Nelson
1663 Liberty Drive
Bloomington, IN 47403
www.westbowpress.com
1-(866) 928-1240

ISBN: 978-1-4908-0230-5 (sc)
ISBN: 978-1-4908-0231-2 (hc)
ISBN: 978-1-4908-0229-9 (e)

Library of Congress Control Number: 2013912769

Printed in the United States of America.

WestBow Press rev. date: 7/29/2013

# DEDICATION

To my daughter, Maisha, who loves, honors,
and respects the Christ in me.

To my late mother, who taught me the value of an intimate
relationship with Jesus Christ.

To my pastor, Leslie Howell, who encouraged me to discover
the untapped potential within me.

# CONTENTS

# PREFACE

Before I became a Christian, I didn't know how to love. I was very defensive; I wouldn't allow anyone entrance into my heart for fear of being hurt. It wasn't until I opened my heart to Jesus that I learned who love is.

For many years, I had heard Christians say there is nothing like intimacy with Christ. I didn't understand what they meant, as He was a stranger within me. I was curious, so I went in pursuit of my new love. I asked spiritually mature Christians what it would take to know Him, and I received the same answers: pray, study the Word, be obedient to the Word, and live a sanctified life. I said to myself, *That sounds easy enough.* Thus began my journey of intimacy.

I made mistakes during my search. I tried to get to know Christ through the lives of other Christians. Big mistake! I observed some who cursed, some who lied, some who deceived, some who fornicated, some who committed adultery, some who drank, and some who stole. I remembered what the Holy Spirit told me at the beginning: pray, study the Word, be obedient to the Word, and live a sanctified life. Frustrated after observing these behaviors, I decided to be obedient and search the Scriptures.

> With the tongue we praise our Lord and Father, and with it we curse men, who have been made in God's likeness.

Out of the same mouth come praise and cursing. My brothers, this should not be. Can both fresh water and salt water flow from the same spring? My brothers, can a fig tree bear olives, or a grapevine bear figs? Neither can a salt spring produce fresh water. (James 3:9-12 NIV)

Through this Scripture, I learned that those who are in Christ do not curse because they have new natures.

Lying lips are extremely disgusting and hateful to the Lord, but they who deal faithfully are His delight. (Proverbs 12:22 AB)

This Scripture proves that God hates liars, so I chose to disagree with lying lips.

What comes out of a person is what defiles them. For it is from within, out of a person's heart, that evil thoughts come—sexual immorality, theft, murder, adultery, greed, malice, *deceit*, lewdness, envy, slander, arrogance, and folly. All these evils come from inside and defile a person. (Mark 7:20-23 NIV, emphasis added)

In these Scriptures, the Lord shows us three sources of sin:

- human nature—out of a person's heart
- human mind—evil thoughts
- human action—sexual immorality, theft, murder, adultery, greed, malice, deceit, lewdness, envy, slander, arrogance, and folly.

I chose to disagree with these sins, which are displeasing to the Lord.

Do you not know that the wicked will not inherit the kingdom of God? Do not be deceived: Neither the sexually immoral [fornicators] nor idolaters nor adulterers nor male prostitutes nor homosexual offenders nor thieves nor the greedy nor drunkards nor slanderers nor swindlers will inherit the kingdom of God. (1 Corinthians 6:9 NIV)

There's more to sex than mere skin on skin. Sex is as much a spiritual mystery as a physical act. As is written in Scripture, "The two become one." Since we want to become spiritually one with the Master, we must never pursue the kind of sex that avoids commitment and intimacy; it will leave us more alone than ever and keep us from ever "becoming one."

In a sense, sexual sins are different from all others. In sexual sin, we violate the sacredness of our bodies, which were made for God-given and God-modeled love, for becoming one with another. We must realize our bodies are sacred places of the Holy Spirit; we cannot live however we please and squander in the process what God paid such a high price for. Our bodies are not pieces of property belonging to the spiritual part of us; God owns the whole works, so let people see God in and through your body (1 Corinthians 6:16-20 MSG).

"So, come out from among [unbelievers], and separate [sever] yourselves from them," says the Lord, "and touch not [any] unclean thing; then I will receive you kindly and treat you with favor, And I will be a Father to you, and you shall be My sons and daughters," says the Lord Almighty. (2 Corinthians 6:17 AB)

I chose to be obedient to the Word of God no matter what behavior other Christians were exhibiting, and out of that obedience came a longing to know Christ and make Him known to others. I began to study the Word and cry out to God every day in prayer to get to know Him better. The Scriptures began to come alive in me. They were not just words in print; they were a living, vital organism.

I decided to make some changes in my life. First, I needed to spend time with Christians who were living the Word. When I took this bold stand, old friends stopped coming around. I was talked about, lied about, betrayed, and misunderstood. I was sad, but I decided to pay whatever price was necessary to know this stranger within.

God sent me new friends who were full of faith. They were bold, confident, and committed to His Word. These women did not compromise the Word of God; they manifested the kingdom of God and were obedient to His Word. These women fascinated me. They spoke the Word boldly, and then things happened. They laid hands on the sick, and the sick were healed. They cast out demons when they spoke the Word, and they changed lives. I wanted what they had by speaking the Word, so I asked them, "How did you become so confident in the Word? They said, "You have to come to a place in your life where you are in an intimate relationship with Jesus." I did not understand what they were saying. I said, "I am born again, but I don't have that special anointing from God that you have." They said, "Yes, you are born again, but that's just the beginning. To reproduce what Jesus manifested on earth, you have to do what He did." They told me, "God is no respecter of persons. You have to consistently seek the Lord every day in prayer and in His Word."

Others had told me to seek the Lord in prayer, to study His Word, to be obedient to his commands, and to live a sanctified life, but they had not told me how important it was to be consistent, so I determined in my heart to consistently seek the Lord. I began asking myself, *Who is this person within me? What is His plan for me? Why is He within me? How will I know Him? What am I supposed to do with Him? Where will He take me?*

People were drawn to Jesus because there was something different about Him. He manifested God on earth, and He pleased the Father in every way. Seeking the Lord will cost you your time, talent, and treasure, but the rewards are far greater than the sacrifice.

We need the Lord; He is what we are searching for. He has created within us that special place for Himself. Humanity has tried to fill that place with drugs, alcohol, pornography, women, men, etc., failing to realize that God created that special place for Himself. Nothing or no one can fill that place except the one for whom it was created.

I wrote this book to encourage others to seek the Lord with their whole spirits, souls, minds, and bodies and not look to others to reveal Christ to them. They must travel alone the road to knowing Him.

Ask yourself, *Do I know Him, or is He a stranger within?*

# INTRODUCTION

When you receive Jesus Christ as your personal Lord and Savior, you are born again. The Holy Spirit of God comes and lives inside you. At that point, He is the stranger within. It is the responsibility of every believer to become intimately acquainted with God's Spirit through His Word and prayer.

"Ask and it will be given to you; seek and you will find; knock and the door will be open to you; For every one who asks receives; he who seeks finds; and to him that knocks, the door will be opened" (Matthew 7:7-8 NIV). Jesus was encouraging the disciples to pray. Our prayers must be based on a relationship with God, who is truly our Father.

"Jesus said to His disciples, 'Could you men not keep watch with me for one hour? Watch and pray so that you will not fall into temptation. The spirit is willing. But the body is weak'" (Matthew 26:40-41 NIV). One hour a day in prayer is a sacrifice most are not willing to pay, but walking with God requires sacrifices. Every day is a new day to be sacrificed to God. Some want to hit and miss, but they will not achieve true intimacy with God through inconsistency. With Jesus, it is all or nothing. When I think about my Lord's sacrifice, one hour a day is a small thing to ask.

"Study to shew thyself approved unto God, a workman that needeth not to be ashamed, rightly dividing the word of truth" (2 Timothy 2:15 KJV). Reading the Bible daily is wonderful. The more you read, the more the Word gets inside you. Reading the Word and studying it are two different activities, however. When you study the Word, you research it until you have a clear understanding of what particular scriptural passages are saying. Studying the Scriptures takes time, but it is amazing how it will cause the Word to come alive and increase understanding.

There is no greater joy than getting to know Christ on the inside; no drug, job, strong drink, man, or woman can compare to Christ Jesus, our resurrected King of Glory.

> Not everyone who says to me, "Lord, Lord" will enter the kingdom of heaven, but only he who does the will of my Father who is in heaven. Many will say to me on that day, "Lord, Lord, did we not prophesy in your name and in your name drive out demons and perform many miracles?" Then I will tell them plainly, "I never knew you. Away from me, you evildoers!" (Matthew 7:21-23 NIV)

Are you pursuing Jesus Christ, or is He a stranger within you?

# CHAPTER 1

# INTIMACY THROUGH THE
# BAPTISM OF THE HOLY SPIRIT

*Those who know their God will seek Him through the
baptism of the Holy Spirit.*

And I will ask the Father, and He will give you another
Comforter [Counselor, Helper, Intercessor, Advocate,
Strengthener, and Standby], that He may remain with you
forever—The Spirit of Truth, Whom the world cannot receive
[welcome, take to its heart], because it does not see Him or
know and recognize Him. But you know and recognize Him,
for He lives with you [constantly] and will be in you.
(John 14:16-17 AB)

Y ou should approach baptism of the Holy Spirit with holy
reverence. When you are baptized in the Holy Spirit, God
will give you the biggest gift in heaven and on earth, Himself.
When you look for God, do not look on the surface; look within.

The ministry of a Christian is the ministry of the Spirit that requires
a surrendered mind and a surrendered life. Salvation is a gift, healing
is a gift, the baptism of the Holy Spirit is a gift, and all are received by
faith. This is why it's wrong to tell people they have to wait to receive

baptism. "Then Peter said unto them, 'Repent, and be baptized every one of you in the name of Jesus Christ for the remission of sins, and ye shall receive the gift of the Holy Ghost'" (Acts 2:38 KJV). Paul wrote, "And be not drunk with wine, wherein is excess; but be filled with the Spirit" (Ephesians 5:18 KJV).

When I was a teenager, I heard people in the Missionary Baptist Church say that tongues were of the Devil, so I naturally grew up fearing the baptism of the Holy Spirit with the evidence of speaking in tongues.

One day, however, my mother left my siblings and me with a family friend while she went out of town to visit my brother in the hospital. While my mother was gone, my friend and I asked her mother if we could meet our boyfriends at a basketball game, and she said yes as long as we attended a church service before the game. We both said, "We can do that." Then she added a stipulation: we had to pay attention and enjoy the service. We thought, *Now she's asking too much.* To go to church was one thing, but to participate in the service was another; however, we agreed because of our plans.

We went to a little backwoods church that had about twenty people in attendance. When the music began, we sang and danced and had such a good time that we forgot about the basketball game. That night, I went to the altar and received the baptism of the Holy Spirit with the evidence of speaking in tongues, and my life changed that night. I entered into a relationship with God I had never known. It was wonderful! All I wanted to do was to be holy and spend more time with the Lord. The passion and fire of God burned in me.

My mother, however, didn't approve of speaking in tongues. She told me, "Them tongues aren't for everyone," and she stopped me from attending the spirit-filled church and made me go back to the

Baptist church. I was so angry and rebellious that I turned away from church. I backslid for about fifteen years, giving no thought to the things of God even though I felt a constant tugging in my heart to return to my first love.

One day, as I was sitting in my bedroom, the presence of the Lord became so strong I could not deny it was Him. He said, "Return to Me," but I answered, "I'm not ready to give up my sinful life" even though deep down inside, I knew someday I would serve Him with my whole heart. The conviction did not leave me until I said yes to the Lord. After months of conviction, I finally repented and returned to God's fold.

Although I repented, the old nature was still stronger than my new life in Christ, and I kept doing what I had been doing before I had been saved. One day, I remembered the vow I had made to the Lord to serve Him with my whole heart. I cried out to God, and He sent a coworker to my house. I explained to her about the vow I had made to the Lord that I had not kept. She said, "You need to be baptized in the Holy Spirit; He will strengthen you for the journey."

I agreed. We knelt down and prayed for the baptism, and tongues gushed out of my mouth. It was as if someone had unleashed a flood of tears. I felt the joy and happiness I had felt at the little church in the woods fifteen years earlier. Since that day, I have never looked back nor have I wanted to go back to that sinful life God had delivered me from. Receiving the baptism of the Holy Spirit was one of the tools I needed to serve the Lord with my whole heart.

Man-made traditions make us think we have to clean up our lives before we can receive the gift of the Holy Spirit. If we could clean up our lives ourselves, would we need the blood of Jesus Christ? We are blood-washed and blood-bought. If we're saved, we're clean. The Holy Spirit ceases to be a gift when we work for it.

When we are born again, our spirits are recreated. If we believe by faith that we are saved, we don't have to do anything but ask and receive.

On the day of Pentecost, Luke said, "They were all filled with the Holy Ghost, and began to speak with other tongues, as the Spirit gave them utterance" (Acts 2:4 KJV). You have to speak; the Holy Spirit will act on your vocal cords, lips, and tongue; He will put supernatural words in your mouth, but you must put the sound into action. The Holy Spirit gives the utterance, but you do the speaking. Forget all the foolishness you may have been taught about speaking in tongues.

> If a son shall ask bread of any of you that is a father, will he give him a stone? Or if he asks a fish, will he for a fish give him a serpent? Or if he shall ask an egg, will he offer him a scorpion? If ye then, being evil, know how to give good gifts unto your children, how much more shall your heavenly Father give the Holy Spirit to them that ask Him? (Luke 11:11-13 KJV)

You have to cooperate with the Holy Spirit, but you don't have to wait anymore, weep, or agonize over it. No other instance is recorded in the Book of Acts after the day of Pentecost that people tarried for the Holy Spirit (Acts 2:4). Peter went to Cornelius's house, and Cornelius and his whole house received the Holy Spirit without waiting (Acts 10). Paul passed through Ephesus, where certain disciples had not heard about the Holy Ghost. He laid hands on them, and they were all filled with the Holy Spirit; none of them waited (Acts 19:1-6). Paul received the Holy Spirit when Ananias laid hands on him (Acts 9:17). Now is the time to receive the water of the Spirit freely!

Open your mouth and tell God, "I am receiving the Holy Spirit right now by faith." Don't speak in English. Relax. Fearlessly and boldly make those supernatural sounds.

# CHAPTER 2

# SEEK YE FIRST THE KINGDOM

*Those who know their God will seek Him through the
kingdom of God first.*

But seek first His Kingdom and His righteousness, and
all these things will be given to you as well.
(Matthew 6:33 NIV)

To *seek* means "to search for." You can't seek God by sitting around and just believing; seeking is an action, not a thought. You have to do something (specifically, pray and read the Word). You have to value your relationship with God more than any earthly relationship. Everything we need is in God's kingdom, but we must first seek Him. We cannot sit around and simply believe the kingdom of God exists; we must pursue God.

Instead of seeking God first, most Christians seek things, treating God as if He were a genie in a bottle who grants every wish, good or bad. Scripture, however, teaches us first things first.

> In those days there appeared John the Baptist, preaching
> in the wilderness [desert] of Judea. And saying, Repent
> [think differently; change your mind, regretting your

sins and changing your conduct], for the kingdom of heaven is at hand. (Matthew 3:1-2 AB)

From that time Jesus began to preach, crying out, "Repent [change your mind for the better, heartily amend your ways, with abhorrence of your past sins], for the kingdom of heaven is at hand." (Matthew 4:17 AB)

The theme of Jesus' preaching was straightforward: He told us to seek the kingdom of God first. He wanted us to realize we should let the complete knowledge of the character of God be most important, before anything else, so the government of God can be established on earth by our lifestyles that reflect His character. When God's character works in us, His kingdom is manifest on earth.

And He went about all Galilee, teaching in their synagogues and preaching the good news [Gospel] of the kingdom, and healing every disease and every weakness and infirmity among the people. (Matthew 4:23 AB)

Having announced that the kingdom of heaven was near, the King declared the principles of that kingdom in His Sermon on the Mount (Matthew 5:1-12).

Jesus reaffirmed that the Mosaic law of the Old Testament's theocratic kingdom was the governing code in His coming kingdom on earth.

Do not think that I have come to abolish the Law or the Prophets; I have not come to abolish them but to fulfill them. I tell you the truth, until heaven and earth disappear, not the smallest letter, not the least stroke of a pen, will by any means disappear from the Law until everything is accomplished. Anyone who breaks one of the least of these commandments and teaches others to do the same will be called least in the kingdom of heaven, but whoever practices and teaches these commands will be called great in the kingdom of heaven. (Matthew 5:17-19 NIV)

Jesus did not come to do away with the law but to fulfill it; He lived in perfect obedience to the law, and by His blood, He mediated the new covenant of grace in which all believers now stand. The law deals with thoughts, motives, overt acts, and hardness of hearts. God's theocratic kingdom will be the rule of the earth.

Although we are not under the law, we must recognize it is a part of the Scriptures, which are inspired of God.

The person who has My commands and keeps them is the one who [really] loves Me; and whoever [really] loves Me will be loved by the Father, and I [too] will love him and will show [reveal, manifest] Myself to him. [I will let myself be clearly seen by him and make myself real to him]. (John 14:21 AB)

Jesus answered, If a person [really] loves me, he will keep my word [obey my teaching]; and My Father will love him, and we will come to him and make our home [abode, special dwelling place] with him. (John 14:23 AB)

If you make God's Word of little importance, you only make yourself of little importance. If you take the Word seriously and show others the way, you will find honor in the kingdom. Your *attitude* toward the Word will determine your *altitude* in the kingdom. God's Word will be working when the stars burn out and the earth wears out.

> But I tell you, Love your enemies and pray for those who persecute you. To show that you are the children of your Father Who is in heaven; for He makes his sun rise on the wicked and on the good, and makes the rain fall upon the upright and the wrongdoers [alike]. For if you love those who love you, what reward can you have? Do not even the tax collectors do that? And if you greet only your brethren what more than others are you doing? Do not even the Gentiles [the heathen] do that? You, therefore, must be perfect [growing into complete maturity of godliness in mind and character, having reached the proper height of virtue and integrity] as your heavenly Father is perfect. (Matthew 5:44-48 AB)

Christ showed us the perfect standard of righteousness demanded by the law. It is time for us to grow up; we are subjects of His kingdom and must begin to act like subjects by living our God-created identities.

"But the fruit of the Spirit is love, joy, peace, longsuffering, gentleness, goodness, faith, meekness, temperance: against such there is no law" (Galatians 5:22-23 KJV). The fruit of the spirit is love, and the other characteristics listed in this Scripture are byproducts of that love. Your fruit can be converts, righteousness, Christian character, and godlike conduct.

There are four stages of fruit bearing: no fruit, fruit, more fruit, and much fruit.

> I am the true vine, and my Father is the gardener. He cuts off every branch in me that bears no fruit, while every branch that does bear fruit He prunes so that it

will be even more fruitful. If a man remains in me and I
in him, he will bear much fruit. (John 15:1-2, 5 NIV)

Bearing no fruit causes God to cut you off. Bearing some fruit is
better than bearing none, but it is not enough for a full life. You
will produce more fruit when you allow God to prune you, and
abiding continuously in Christ will allow you to yield much fruit.
God prunes us by His Word so we can bear much fruit. When we
are not in Christ, we are deadwood, good only for the fire, but if we
remain in Him, we will have unbroken fellowship and communion
with Him.

Fruit grows as a result of life. First comes the bud, then the blossom,
and finally the fruit. Fruit is impossible where there is death. The
fruit of the Spirit is the direct result of the life of Christ ministered
to believers by the Spirit. Loss of communion with God is one of the
reasons people fail to produce spiritual fruit; no amount of Christian
work or even the exercise of spiritual gifts such as teaching can
substitute for walking with God.

Many see the fruit of the Spirit in the wrong way. They go to camp
meetings or conventions or to a special preacher to seek blessings,
thinking that the fruit they desire will be suddenly implanted in their
natures. Unless they walk with Christ, however, they are doomed to
disappointment.

We must meet three conditions to achieve a fruitful life:

**We must be cleansed.** "If we confess our sins, He is faithful and just
to forgive us our sins, and to cleanse us from all unrighteousness" (1
John 1:9 NIV). We are cleansed from all sin once and for all by the
blood of Jesus, but throughout our earthly life, we need to confess
our daily sins to the Father so we can abide in unbroken fellowship

with Him. Christ will not have communion with a defiled saint, but He can and will cleanse us.

**We must remain in the vine.** "If you remain in me [the true vine] and my words remain in you, ask whatever you wish and it will be given you" (John 15:7 NIV). We can take all our burdens to Christ and draw wisdom, life, and strength from Him; we can't allow anything to separate us from Him.

**We must be obedient.** "If you obey my commands, you will remain in my love, just as I have obeyed my Father's commands and remain in His love. My command is this: Love each other as I have loved you" (John 15:10, 12 NIV). There is real power in the fruit of the Spirit that comes from communion and not crises.

The new law of Christ is divine love in our hearts renewed by the Holy Spirit; it flows unforced and spontaneously in contrast to the external law of Moses, which demands love. Christ's law is love, and it is written on our hearts.

We need to relax and not be preoccupied with getting so we can respond to God's giving. Those who don't know God fuss over things, while those who know Him remain at peace, knowing He will provide all we require.

When we trust God and seek His kingdom first, He will be with us in good and bad times. As we develop this trust in God's faithfulness, He will no longer be a stranger within.

# CHAPTER 3

# INTIMACY THROUGH FAITH

*Those who know their God will seek Him through
the intimacy of faith.*

Now we see but a poor reflection as in a mirror; then we shall
see face to face. Now I now in part; then I shall know fully,
even as I am fully known. And now these three remain; faith,
hope and love. But the greatest of these is love.
(1 Corinthians 13:12-13 NIV)

I was awakened one morning by a voice that asked, "Do you
know Him, or is He a stranger within?" To come to Jesus, we
have to believe He is who He says He is, and that begins with
faith. We have to realize the difference between faith and belief.

## WHAT IS FAITH?

Now faith is the assurance [the confirmation, the title
deed] of the things [we] hope for, being the proof of
things [we] do not see and the conviction of their reality
[faith perceiving as real fact what is not revealed to the
senses]. (Hebrews 11:1 AB)

> Now faith is the substance [ultimate reality that underlies all outward manifestations and change] of things hoped for, the evidence of things not seen. (Hebrews 11:1 AB)

*Substance* is evidence that something exists. In the case of faith, substance is the evidence that the hoped-for things exist although we do not see them.

Faith is God's foundation, which means we can lean on Him, we can pick up our troubles and slam them on Him, we can hide in the cleft of the rock Jesus Christ, and we can trust in the throes of extreme pain on a strand of rope twisted into a great rope made strong.

*Webster's* definition of faith is being certain of, having full trust and complete confidence in, without doubt or question, whether there be evidence or not. Faith for salvation is personal trust in the Lord Jesus Christ, who was delivered up for our offenses and raised again for our justification. "For God so loved the world that He gave His one and only Son, that whoever believes in him shall not perish but have eternal life" (John 3:16 NIV). Faith used in prayer is the assurance we have in approaching God that if we ask anything according to His will, He will hear us: "This is the confidence we have in approaching God: that if we ask anything according to His will, He hears us. And if we know that He hears us—whatever we ask—we know that we have what we asked of Him" (1 John 5:14 NIV). Those of us who are parents do not give our children everything they want; we give them what is best for them. God knows everything about us and knows how to get us to our destination.

Faith gives substance to the unseen so that it becomes reality. In Genesis 1, God said, "Let there be light," and there was light. My pastor always says how you see determines your destiny. We have to see through the eyes of faith.

To continually grow in grace and favor with God and man, we must be connected to a church and submit to a pastor so we can be fed the Word of God and assemble with other believers: "And I will give you pastors according to mine heart, which shall feed you with knowledge and understanding" (Jeremiah 3:15 KJV). "So then faith cometh by hearing, and hearing by the word of God" (Romans 10:17 KJV).

I had a vision while praying: I was in my house, working on a task my pastor had assigned me. I heard loud screams coming from outside. I saw some Christians and non-Christians, some houses, a car, and furnishings in water about eight or so feet deep. As I gazed at this sight, a flash of lightning hit the water, frying everything and everyone in the water. Though the water was higher than my house, it did not enter it; it was as if an invisible barrier were holding it back. I asked God why the water had not entered my garage, and He responded, "My wrath and judgment are coming to this earth. You represent Christians who are connected to a church, who have submitted to a pastor, and who are doing what God has called them to do. Those who perished represent people who are doing their own thing with no accountability or connection to a pastor."

God places pastors in the body of Christ to feed His sheep. We need to hear the Word of the Lord from those He has called and anointed to preach the Word; this builds our faith.

## What Is Belief?

Belief is reliance upon or trust in a person or object; it is receiving what God has revealed. *Webster's* definition of belief is to "mentally accept as truth; conviction based on examination or evidence." We have taken for granted that faith and belief are the same, just two ways of saying the same thing; however, even though they are alike in meaning, they are not the same: "For [if we are] in Christ Jesus, neither circumcision nor uncircumcision counts for anything, but only faith activated and energized and expressed and working through love" (Galatians 5:6 AB).

Love motivates, and faith activates. Love pushes us forward, and faith drives us to action. Faith operates through love. Many people think they know what it is to walk by faith, but if you carefully examine their lives and what is coming out of their mouths, you will see they do not walk by faith.

Your faith prompts you to act on what you believe. If you do not act on what you believe, you will not be able to change your circumstances, because faith is what changes your circumstances. You may say, "I don't know if I can stand it any longer" or "I cannot take anymore," but you should always remember that God allows the fire to see if you really trust Him and His Word.

> Peter said, [You should] be exceedingly glad on this account, though now for a little while you may be distressed by trials and suffer temptations, So that [the genuineness] of your faith may be tested, [your faith] which is infinitely more precious than the perishable gold which is tested and purified by fire. [This proving of your faith is intended] to redound to [lead to] [your] praise and glory and honor when Jesus Christ [the Messiah, the Anointed One] is revealed. (1 Peter 1:6-7 AB)

As a believer, you have the greatest opportunity right now, for the darker the outlook, the more difficult the adversity, the greater the problem, the more God can be glorified.

Believing is where you start, but it's not where you stop, because you get nothing from just believing. Even though everything you believe is true, you have to act on it: "But be ye doers of the word, and not hearers only, deceiving your own selves" (James 1:22 KJV). The Word will not benefit you if you sit in service after service hearing the Word but not doing what it says—*faith* is an action word.

If God said it, that settles it. Truth does not depend on whether we believe it, and experiencing the truth does depend on whether we act on it. Jesus exercised His authority. We cannot just think about the authority we have; we have to act on it. Jesus' faith was activated by doing something, not just believing. Our faith has to be activated by acting on what we believe. If we truly trust and believe in God, we will not fear, which is false evidence that appears real but is the opposite of faith. Intimacy with God comes through faith in Him, and faith in Him means He is no longer a stranger within but a friend.

## Confession

I repent of doubt and unbelief, and I thank You for being faithful and just to forgive me. I receive Your supernatural, abundant faith in Jesus' name.

# CHAPTER 4

# INTIMACY THROUGH HOPE

*Those who know their God will seek Him through
the intimacy of hope.*

May the God of hope fill you with all joy and peace as you
trust in him, so that you may overflow with hope
by the power of the Holy Spirit.
(Romans 15:13 NIV)

Webster's definition of hope is "to cherish; a desire with expectation of fulfillment; to long for with expectation of obtainment; to expect with desire; trust." Hope means looking forward to what you desire with expectation.

> Therefore, remember that formerly you who are Gentiles by birth and called "uncircumcised" by those who call themselves "the circumcision" (that done in the body by the hands of men)—remember that at that time you were separate from Christ, excluded from citizenship in Israel and foreigners to the covenants of the promise, without God in the world. But now in Christ Jesus you who once were far away have been brought near through the blood of Christ. (Ephesians 2:11-13 NIV)

Biblical hope is a certainty, a confident expectation of what God will do in the future based on His past faithfulness and promises. "My soul finds rest, O my soul, in God alone; my hope comes from Him. He alone is my rock and my salvation; He is my fortress, I will not be shaken" (Psalm 62:1-2 NIV).

Your soul is at rest when you truly know and trust God, knowing He is in control.

> We have this hope as an anchor for the soul, firm and secure. It enters the inner sanctuary behind the curtain, where Jesus, who went before us, has entered on our behalf. He has become a high priest forever, in the order of Melchizedek. (Hebrews 6:19-20 NIV)

Our hope is certain if we know and have faith in what Jesus Christ has done and is still doing for us. Jesus is the object of our hope in a world that has no hope.

> We also rejoice in our sufferings, because we know that suffering produces perseverance; perseverance, character; and character, hope. And hope does not disappoint us, because God has poured out His love into our hearts by the Holy Spirit, whom He has given us. (Romans 5:3-5 NIV)

We can face adversity and trials with courage and joy because we know our hope is in God and His Word, which lasts forever; our hope in Him gives us pleasure.

> He gives strength to the weary and increases the power of the weak. Even youths grow tired and weary, and young men stumble and fall; but those who hope in the

Lord will renew their strength. They will soar on wings like eagles; they will run and not grow weary, they will walk and not be faint. (Isaiah 40:29-31 NIV)

The Lord rewards those who confidently wait upon Him. There was a time in my life when I became discouraged because I was not in full-time ministry as my friends were. One day, a man of God told me, "Things are not what they appear to be. It may appear as though you are not progressing spiritually. However, continue waiting on the Lord and allow Him to perfect you. If you do that, you will soar past them all." Our waiting includes the conviction that God is supreme. Desire is the hunger and thirst after righteousness, and hope is joy flowing from our faith that those desires will be fulfilled.

> But the eyes of the Lord are on those who fear Him, on those whose hope is in His unfailing love, to deliver them from death and keep them alive in famine. We wait in hope for the Lord. He is our help and our shield. In Him our hearts rejoice, for we trust in His holy name. May your unfailing love rest upon us, O Lord, even as we put our hope in you. (Psalm 33:18-22 NIV)

Our reliance and confidence must be in God alone because He is everything to us. The grace of hope causes us to trust in the Lord.

> Out of the depths I cry to you, O Lord; O Lord, hear my voice. Let your ears be attentive to my cry for mercy. If you, O Lord, kept a record of sins, O Lord, who could stand? But with you there is forgiveness; therefore you are feared. I wait for the Lord, my soul waits, and in His word I put my hope. My soul waits for the Lord more than watchmen wait for the morning. More than watchmen wait for the morning, O Israel, put your hope

in the Lord, for with the Lord is unfailing love and with
Him is full redemption. (Psalm 130:1-7 NIV)

Our posture should be humble and forgiving while we are waiting,
hoping, and watching.

Forgiveness will humble us. With a heart of forgiveness, we must not
forget that we have been pardoned from our sins. We should show
our brothers and sisters the same loving-kindness Jesus showed us.
We must wait on God by faith and have hope in His Word. God has
His own time for giving, and what He gives is worth the wait.

True believers hope, wait, and trust the Lord because they know
Him as Lord. He is no longer a stranger within to them.

# CHAPTER 5

# INTIMACY THROUGH LOVE

*Those who know their God will seek Him through
the intimacy of love.*

Therefore, as God's chosen people, holy and dearly loved,
clothe yourselves with compassion, kindness, humility,
gentleness and patience. Bear with each other and forgive
whatever grievances you may have against one another.
Forgive as the Lord forgave you. And over all these virtues put
on love, which binds them all together in perfect unity.
(Colossians 3:12-14 NIV)

There are three Greek words in the Bible that mean love:
*eros*, *phileo*, and *agape*. Eros means strong passion; this is
not the kind of love God expects from His people. Passion
does have its place in a marriage, but ungovernable intoxication with
another person is foreign to the Bible.

Phileo means a genuine friendship or kindness based on a relationship
of fondness; it is also translated as "brotherly love."

Agape means the God kind of love. It is a determination of the will
to prefer something.

*Webster's* definition of love is "to cherish; to feel a passion, devotion, or tenderness for; to take pleasure in." When the Bible speaks of love, it is not talking about natural love. Divine love comes from the new life we have in Christ Jesus, from which all spiritual fruit grows. Natural love loves its own; it flourishes in an atmosphere of friendship and is fed by mutual affection. Only on rare occasions will natural love persist when it is not returned. Love that flows from the spirit goes beyond natural love. It causes us to love our enemies and do good to those who despitefully use us. "If you love those who love you, what credit is that to you?" (Luke 6:32 NIV).

As we look at the life of Jesus Christ, we can see God's character of love exhibited through Him. "The fruit of the Spirit is love, joy, peace, patience, kindness, goodness, faithfulness, gentleness and self-control, goodness, faith, meekness, temperance" (Galatians 5:22-23 NLT).

The fruit of the Spirit is a portrait of Christ. Spiritual fruit is the outcome of a life of unbroken and full communion with Christ.

> Abide in me, and I in you. As the branch cannot bear
> fruit of itself, except it abide in the vine, no more can ye,
> except ye abide in me. I am the vine, ye are the branches;
> He that abideth in me, and I in him, the same bringeth
> forth much fruit; for without me ye can do nothing.
> (John 15:4-5 KJV)

Christ within us can accomplish what we can never hope to do relying on our own strength; continuous walking with Him will change the weakest of us into His image. His life in us will make love grow. First comes the bud, then the blossom, and finally the fruit. The fruit of love is impossible where there is death.

Love is the direct result of the life of Christ ministered to believers by the Spirit, and loss of communion with God is one reason believers fail to walk in love. Real spiritual power comes from the love of God and not from crises. The maximum manifestation of spiritual power is achieved only when love and gifts work together. The greatest example of the two working together is our Lord Jesus Christ.

In 1 Corinthians 13, we read about how love never fails and about how prophecies, tongues, and knowledge will pass away, but three will remain: faith, hope, and love.

"Eagerly pursue and seek to acquire [this] love [make it your aim] and cultivate the spiritual endowments [gifts]" (1 Corinthians 14:1 AB).

Love does not change when our situations change: Jesus said at Golgotha, "Father, forgive them, for they do not know what they are doing" (Luke 23:34 NIV). Stephen prayed as his enemies stoned him to death, "Lord, lay not this sin to their charge" (Acts 7:60 KJV). Even after Peter denied Christ, Jesus still loved him (Matthew 26:69-70). Love has to be sacrificial. Natural love may sacrifice for the one it loves, but divine love goes beyond caring about loved ones.

> Very rarely will anyone die for a righteous man, though for a good man someone might possibly dare to die. But God demonstrates His own love for us in this: While we were still sinners, Christ died for us. (Romans 5:7-8 NIV)

Divine love makes the supreme sacrifice for those who are unworthy, and it extends even to their enemies. Love can be tough but necessary at times. Natural love breaks down when it deals with chastisement, but divine love builds up. Whom the Lord loves he chastens.

In 2 Corinthians 13, Paul encouraged the Corinthian believers to examine and test themselves to see if they were in the faith. Paul used his authority to build them up, which required divine love.

Love given by the Holy Spirit is above our personal interests. The truth means more than all ties of natural affection.

The old saying, "Love is blind," may be true about natural love but certainly not about agape love—agape love keeps its eyes open to everything, acts accordingly, and keeps on loving.

> Therefore, as God's chosen people, holy and dearly loved, clothe yourselves with compassion, kindness, humility, gentleness and patience. Bear with each other and forgive whatever grievances you may have against one another. Forgive as the Lord forgave you. And over all these virtues put on love, which binds them all together in perfect unity. (Colossians 3:12-14 NIV)

The church contains such a diversity of personality that unity seems impossible, but God's divine love can achieve it. Someday, the gifts will pass away, but not until their work is done. That day will come only when the final full manifestation of the fruit of love is mature in all God's children. When we meet our Lord, shining above all will be love.

## REPEAT

I am patient.
I am kind.
I don't envy.
I don't boast.

I am not proud.
I am not rude.
I am not self-seeking.
I am not easily angered.
I keep no record of wrongs.
I don't delight in evil.
I rejoice with the truth.
I always protect.
I always trust.
I always hope.
I always persevere.
I never fail because I am Love.

When the love of God is not manifest in our lives, He remains a stranger within. It is impossible to know Him who is love and not manifest His love.

# CHAPTER 6

# INTIMACY THROUGH HOLINESS

*Those who know their God will seek Him through
the intimacy of holiness.*

But just as He who called you is holy, so be holy in all you do;
for it is written: Be holy, because I am Holy.
(1 Peter 1:15-16 NIV)

Throughout the Scriptures, the Lord admonishes us to be holy. Holiness is purity; freedom from anything that contaminates, weakens, or pollutes; it is innocence. To live holy lives, we must separate ourselves from the influences of this world and be totally committed to the Lord. Those of us who are intimately acquainted with God will walk in holiness.

*Webster's* defines holiness as an essential characteristic we must recognize as a condition of the mind. Holiness is an inherited characteristic that sets us apart from sin for one purpose: to serve God and bring honor to Him. David wrote Psalm 101, a vow for a holy life, because he knew he was going to become king. Chosen of the Lord, David purposed to live a holy life: "I will sing of your love and justice; to you, O Lord, I will sing praise" (Psalm 101:1 NIV).

David praised God for His love and His discipline—the sweet and the bitter. We should bless the Lord for His judgment, which chastens our sin, and for his mercy, which forgives it. We should admire the goodness and the justice of God because what we admire we tend to imitate. No matter what others do, we must praise the Lord. "I will be careful to lead a blameless life. When will you come to me?" (Psalm 101:2a NIV).

To be holy is to be wise. If you don't purpose in your heart to live a holy life, you will do evil. "For evildoers shall be cut off, but those who wait and hope and look for the Lord [in the end] shall inherit the earth" (Psalm 37: 9 AB).

Don't allow sin to enter your life while you are waiting upon God. Some Christians give up just before their breakthroughs. Remember that God is faithful; He may not respond when we want Him to, but He will respond. "When will you come to me? I will walk in my house with a blameless heart" (Psalm 101:2b, c NIV).

Godly service begins at home. If our hearts are not perfect at home, they will not be perfect away from home. We must not sing in the choir and sin in the chamber; we should not be saints outside the home and devil inside the home. A true saint and a faithful minister is one who is respected at home. We should ask ourselves, *Do those in my home dread it when I come home?*

"I will set before my eyes no vile thing" (Psalm 101:3a NIV). Protect your eyes and ears by being careful about what you watch and listen to. Your eyes and ears are gates that give entrance to the soul to things that are good or bad.

"The deeds of faithless men I hate; they will not cling to me" (Psalm 101:3b NIV). Hatred of sin is essential to virtue. We must take the high road of integrity instead of the crooked way of sin. We should never be like those who deviate from the way of righteousness: "So come out from among [unbelievers], and separate [sever] yourselves from them, says the Lord, and touch not [any] unclean thing; then I will receive you kindly and treat you with favor" (2 Corinthians 6:17 AB). We must separate ourselves from whatever is contrary to the mind of God and cling to God Himself. We must separate our desires, motives, and acts from those of the world. It's impossible for God to bless and use us if we compromise the gospel and associate with evil.

Separation does not mean having no contact with evil in the world or even in the church; it means not partaking of or conforming to it. There has to be something different about us that makes sinners want what we have, Jesus. We cannot imitate the world and abide in the Lord. Our reward for separation will be unhindered communion and worship with God and fruitful service. We must always remember that Jesus Christ is our "prototype," an original model, an archetype, the original pattern of behavior, belief, and faith we should emulate. Jesus is holy, blameless, and pure. He was in the world but not of the world.

"Men of perverse heart shall be far from me; I will have nothing to do with evil" (Psalm 101:4 NIV). We should never associate with those who have evil characters. When our hearts are pure, we will not tolerate evil companions. We should never throw them away; we should just tell them we do not approve of their ways. If we run with the wicked, we'll soon be known as wicked, as like spirits travel together.

> [Live] as children of obedience [to God]; do not conform yourselves to the evil desires [that governed you] in your former ignorance [when you did not know

the requirements of the Gospel]. But as the One who called you is holy, you yourselves also be holy in all your conduct and manner of living. For it is written, You shall be holy, for I am holy. (1 Peter 1:14-16 AB)

We must get over the mind-set that we cannot live holy lives. God requires us to be holy; that means we can indeed live holy lives.

"Whoever slanders his neighbor in secret, him will I put to silence" (Psalm 101:5a NIV).

To stab a neighbor in the back is brutal, cruel, and wicked. It amazes me how many believers sin in private and think God does not see them. God is omnipresent; He is everywhere and sees everything.

"He who hides hatred is of lying lips, and he who utters slander is a [self-confident] fool" (Proverbs 10:18 AB). The Lord hates liars and everything that is false. As my mother said, if you cannot say something good about a person, do not say anything at all.

"Whoever has haughty eyes and a proud heart, him will I not endure" (Psalm 101:5b NIV). You can't look down on those who are less fortunate than you; a proud heart is a hard heart unfit for the Lord's service.

"Pride goes before destruction and a haughty spirit before a fall" (Proverbs 16:18 NIV). One who walks in pride will soon fall.

"My eyes will be on the faithful in the land that they may dwell with me" (Psalm 101:6a NIV). A faithful servant is a treasure; God will seek out the faithful in the land. He will take care of them and promote them to positions of honor. When we are unfaithful to God, He will be unfaithful to us.

"To the faithful you show yourself faithful" (Psalm 18:25a NIV). "He whose walk is blameless will minister to me" (Psalm 101:6b NIV). God doesn't sanction persons of bad character. The unsaved should value us because of our walks whether they agree with us or not. "To the blameless you show yourself blameless, to the pure you show yourself pure, but to the devious you show yourself shrewd" (Psalm 18:25b-26a NIV).

"No one who practices deceit will dwell in my house" (Psalm 101:7a NIV). You can be sure your sins will find you out. You can attempt to hide sin from men, but you cannot hide sin from God. You must set yourself against sin.

"No one who speaks falsely will stand in my presence" (Psalm 101:7b NIV). Liars should not be in our sight or hearing. Grace makes us truthful and causes us to hate lies.

"Lying lips are extremely disgusting and hateful to the Lord, but they who deal faithfully are His delight" (Proverbs 12:22 AB). The Lord will not countenance the sight of liars; those who love to lie will not attain heaven. Liars are offensive enough on earth; we are not going to be worried about them in heaven.

"Every morning I will put to silence all the wicked in the land" (Psalm 101:8a NIV). "All the horns of the ungodly also will I cut off [says the Lord], but the horns of the [uncompromisingly] righteous shall be exalted" (Psalm 75:10 AB). The Lord is not unjust; He bids us to leave our sin so He can pardon us. He suffers long and is kind even to those who are wicked, but He will be a terror to the wicked if they don't change their ways. "I will cut off every evildoer from the city of the Lord" (Psalm 101:8b NIV).

Judgment will begin at the house of the Lord. It's a serious thing to be called a Christian. When we bring reproach upon the name of Jesus, we injure not only ourselves but also others. We must walk before the Lord with a pure heart.

Some of the benefits we will receive for walking in holiness:

> He will live in us.
> He will walk with us.
> He will be our God, and we will be His sons and daughters.
> He will accept us into the beloved.
> He will be our Father.

Why must we walk in holiness? Because everything associated with God is holy.

> His dwelling is holy.
> His name is holy.
> His throne is holy.
> His power is holy.
> His Word is holy.
> His ways are holy.

Everything about God is free from sin; therefore, those of us who draw near to Him must be holy. "For we know that our old self [our corrupt human nature, the inborn tendency to do evil] was crucified with him so that the body of sin might be done away with [rendered powerless], that we should no longer be slaves to sin" (Romans 6:6 NIV). That old life died with Christ on the cross and no longer has power over us. We now have the Holy Spirit, who gives us new life and strengthens us. When we follow the Holy Spirit, we are the kind of people God wants us to be.

How great is the love the Father has lavished on us, that we should be called children of God! And that is what we are! The reason the world does not know us is that it did not know Him. Dear friends, now we are children of God, and what we will be has not yet been made known. But we know that when He appears, we shall be like Him, for we shall see him as He is. Everyone who has this hope in Him purifies himself, just as He is pure. (1 John 3:1-3 NIV)

Holiness is the next wave of God. It will do some deep cleansing in our lives to prepare us for His coming. We will be tried in the fire until everything not of God is burned up. This purging will not be easy; it will be very painful. God is going to allow circumstances to come into our lives to bring to the surface hidden attitudes of our hearts—unholy thoughts, actions, and relationships. There will be no more hypocrisy, saying one thing and doing another. Holiness will be manifest in our conversation, thoughts, attitudes, and relationships.

To live in holiness:

- Ask God to expose sin in your life as David did (Psalm 19:12-14).
- Present yourself to God so He can cut away everything not holy (Romans 12:1-2).
- Break unholy alliances with the world (James 4:4).
- Reject ungodly attitudes and desires (Galatians 5:19-21).
- Cleanse yourself from ungodly lifestyles (2 Corinthians 6:14-7:1).
- Make God's Word your standard of obedience (James 1:22-25).
- Be accountable (Hebrews 4:12-13).

- Renew your first love (Revelation 2:4-5).
- Keep your focus on eternity (Hebrews 11:24-26).

In the midst of this evil generation, God has called us to walk in holiness. Jesus is not coming for a harlot bride who has been committing spiritual adultery with the world, nor is He coming for a bride who has become polluted with the sinful lusts and desires of this world. He is coming for a holy, end-time remnant, a people who have been cleansed and purified, those without spot or blemish.

Examine your life today:

- Have you been deceived by what is considered but is not righteous?
- Are you comfortable with sin?
- Have you allowed God to transform your sinful nature to reflect His holy nature?
- Are you still living after the dictates of the world, the flesh, and the Devil?

We are a holy people unto God, and a holy life is essential to knowing and abiding with God. God is still a stranger within those of us who choose to live as the Devil does in conduct and manner.

## CHAPTER 7

# INTIMACY THROUGH WORSHIP

*Those who know their God will seek Him through
the intimacy of worship.*

Yet a time is coming and has now come when the true
worshipers will worship the Father in spirit and truth, for they
are the kind of worshipers the Father seeks. God is a spirit and
his worshipers must worship in spirit and truth.
(John 4:23-24 NIV)

To worship God in spirit is to worship Him from the heart.
To worship Him in truth, we must come to Him through
His Word, Jesus, the way.

The word *worship* is a short form of *worthship*. Used as a verb,
it means to ascribe worth or to acknowledge value. To worship
God is to recognize His worth or worthiness, to look to Him and
acknowledge His value in all appropriate ways. *Webster's* definition
of worship is "to honor or reverence as a divine being; to regard
with great, even extravagant respect, honor, or devotion." To the
world, worship is tedious and boring, but to Christians, worship
is a joy.

## Worship through Prayer

True intimacy is birthed in prayer. "Pray without ceasing" (1 Thessalonians 5:17 KJV). Prayer begins with desire, or longing, to know Jesus, and *Webster's* defines desire as a longing, a delight. "As the hart pants and longs for the water brooks, so I pant and long for you O God. My inner self thirsts for God, for the living God. When shall I come and behold the face of God?" (Psalm 42:1-2 AB).

Prayer is meant to be one of the most exciting aspects of a life of faith. Some have not come before the throne of God but believe they are nonetheless in an intimate relationship with Christ. There can be no intimacy with Christ, however, until they come before the throne of God. Those who have experienced God's presence around the throne are changed; no one can come into God's presence and remain the same.

Prayer is a mystery some do not understand. Some believers pray without believing, while others pray as a ritual, with no reality. Some have been discouraged because their prayers have seemed to be fruitless rituals with no evidence of tangible results, while many more have quit praying. Jesus, however, encourages us to pray. "Ask and it will be given to you; seek and you will find; knock and the door will be opened to you. For everyone who asks receives; he who seeks finds; and to him who knocks, the door will be opened" (Matthew 7:7-8 NIV).

- Ask: to call for, crave, desire, demand something due.
- Seek: to worship, desire, require to find.
- Find: to get, obtain, perceive, see.
- Knock: to overcome.

- Open: to make available for entry, to make available for or active in a regular function, to make accessible for a particular purpose.

Who and what is the door? "Jesus said, 'I am the gate; whoever enters through me will be saved. He will come in and go out, and find pasture.' He also said, 'I am the way and the truth and the life. No one comes to the Father except through me'" (John 14:6 NIV).

- Prayer is our training ground where we prepare to reign with Jesus.
- Prayer is mankind giving God the legal right and permission to intervene in earth's affairs.
- Prayer is man giving heaven license to influence earth.
- Prayer is the vehicle by which we commune and communicate with God.
- Prayer is calling into being what God has already purposed and predestined.

If my people, who are called by my name, will humble themselves and pray and seek my face and turn from their wicked ways, then will I hear from heaven and will forgive their sin and will heal their land. (2 Chronicles 7:14 NIV)

I will give you the keys of the kingdom of heaven; whatever you bind on earth will be bound in heaven, and whatever you loose on earth will be loosed in heaven. (Matthew 16:19 NIV)

These Scriptures give mankind the authority and prerogative to determine what happens on earth. God does nothing on earth without the cooperation of a person. To preserve mankind during the flood, He needed Noah. To create a nation, He needed Abraham. To lead the nation of Israel out of bondage, He needed Moses. To free Israel from captivity, He needed Daniel. To defeat Jericho, He needed Joshua. To preserve the Hebrews, He needed Esther. To save mankind, He needed to become a man.

God does nothing but in answer to prayer. Heaven needs us to give it license to impact earth. Prayer builds intimacy with God, it brings honor to His nature and character, it causes us to trust in His love, it affirms His purposes, and it appropriates His promises.

"When you ask, you do not receive, because you ask with wrong motives, that you may spend what you get on your pleasures" (James 4:3 NIV). Prayer is meant to be answered; otherwise, God would not ask us to pray. Everything we need to fulfill our purposes is available to us. Through prayer, we may receive all that God is and all that He has. If we ask for that which is contrary to God's purposes for us, we will be frustrated. Jesus always prayed for God's will to be done and then worked to accomplish His will.

Jesus expressed His confidence that God heard His prayers: "Then Jesus looked up and said, 'Father, I thank you that you have heard me. I knew that you always hear me, but I said this for the benefit of the people standing here, that they may believe that you sent me'" (John 11:41-42 NIV). Whatever we pray for, whether it is for the needs of an individual, family, community, nation, or world, we must seek to be in agreement with God's will so His purpose can be manifest on earth. When we stop praying, we allow God's purposes for the world to be hindered. Prayer is not an option for believers—it is a right, a privilege, and a necessity.

Jesus is our model of dominion and authority on earth. God revealed to Jesus what He was doing in the world and how Jesus' ministry related to His overall purpose. Jesus' prayers were effective because He had a relationship with God, knew His purpose, and prayed according to God's will. When we are in relationship with the Lord, we will know our purpose. This will take away doubt, fear, uncertainty, and timidity concerning prayer. We can pray, and we have to pray, expecting to be heard. Jesus always kept a close relationship with the Father through prayer.

God does not want us to use Him as "fire insurance" to keep us out of hell. We should have a healthy fear of God and keep His commandments, but He wants a relationship, not a religion. Before we can truly enter His presence, we must express our love for Him through intimacy by entering into His mind and heart and becoming one with Him in purpose.

Prayer is more important than all the other activities of the day. Through prayer, God gives guidance, wisdom, and discernment for fulfilling His will and purpose. Prayer is the only thing the disciples asked Jesus to teach them. Why do you think they made this request? Because they saw what He did as a result of the hours he spent in prayer. He spent four or five hours in prayer but only a few seconds casting out demons and healing the sick.

We must free ourselves from all our hindrances to answered prayer such as sin, fear, guilt, feelings of inferiority, doubt, wrong motives, bitterness, unforgiveness, broken family relationships, idols, and stinginess.

Praying in the name of Jesus gives our prayers tremendous power. Using Jesus' name does not mean we can pray any type of prayer we want and say, "In the name of Jesus, amen" 'prayer does not work that way. Jesus' name is not a magic formula that guarantees automatic acceptance of all our prayers. We must be able to use legitimately the power of Jesus' name based on our covenant relationship with God through Christ. Jesus' name is the only name that can activate power in heaven. Let us all remember that heaven, our families, the earth, our children, and all creation depend on us to pray. Let us also remember that the Devil hates our prayer lives because he does not want us to learn who God is, who we are, and what purposes God has for our lives.

To know God, we have to walk with Him in that secret place. One day, while I was praying, I asked God to reveal Himself to me. I was suddenly in a dark room with a door. The only light in the room was coming from around the door. I walked over to the door, which opened by itself. I found myself in a beautiful garden with mist coming from the ground. As I stood there casting off fear, I began to confess I was not afraid of God's presence because I had been in His presence before He had shot me into this world. I started thanking Him for allowing me to be in His presence. The Lord grabbed my hand and said, "Stop talking and walk with me."

As we walked, we were silent, but my body tingled as if it were on fire. As we walked, I finally got the revelation that our transformation comes from walking with God not by words or deeds but by simply being in His presence; that is what allows us to receive whatever we need to be like Him.

When we "walk" with God, we become like Him in our conduct, behavior, and attitude. Walking with God also means moving into a heavenly realm outside the ordinary restrictions or boundaries set in time and place, away from the world of human, physical experience, and free from the control or restrictions of our lives.

## WORSHIP THROUGH THE WORD

> Do not let this Book of the Law depart from your mouth; meditate on it day and night, so that you may be careful to do everything written in it. Then you will be prosperous and successful. (Joshua 1:8 NIV)

> Blessed is the man who does not walk in the counsel of the wicked or stand in the way of sinners or sit in the seat of mockers. But his delight is in the law of the Lord and on his law he meditates day and night. (Psalm 1:1-2 NIV)

> Do your best to present yourself to God as one approved, a workman who does not need to be ashamed and who correctly handles the word of truth.
> (2 Timothy 2:15 NIV)

The only book the Lord allowed me to read for approximately two years was His Word. Studying and reading the Word daily allowed me to grow spiritually. I received a lot of criticism from older believers who refused to believe God was transforming my life so quickly, but their criticism did not stop me; my hunger for God's Word and presence far outweighed their criticism.

The Word of God will:

- become your meat. Chew, swallow, bring up again; chew, swallow, and bring up again until you believe and obey what is written;
- become your lifestyle. It will become so much a part of you that you will find it strange when others do not feast on it daily;

- become your daily fuel that energizes you. Speak the Word only; anything else you dare not utter;
- transform you. We are what we eat, and we manifest what we feast on; and
- illuminate you and cause you to shine forth as the noonday sun. All will see that light and be drawn to it. You will be that light on a hill that cannot be hidden.

My advice to every believer is to abide in the Word and let it abide in you. Do not allow the Devil to deceive you; abiding in the Word daily and doing what it commands will transform you.

> For the Word that God speaks is alive and full of power [making it active, operative, energizing, and effective]; it is sharper than any two-edged sword, penetrating to the dividing line of the "breath of life (soul) and [the immortal] spirit, and of joints and marrow [of the deepest parts of our nature], exposing and sifting and analyzing and judging the very thoughts and purposes of the heart. (Hebrews 4:12 AB)

The Word is a living organism that gives health to our bodies. We must allow ourselves to be lost in the Word so we can be found in Christ, who is the Word. One day, while praying, I saw myself go inside Jesus' body. I could no longer see myself—just Jesus. God's will is that none of us be seen, only Him. The Word is the transforming agent we need to look just like Jesus.

John 17 contains Jesus' high priestly prayer to His Father. This prayer reveals the heart of the Son of God. Jesus is God's love gift to us, and we are God's love gift to Him.

Neither for these alone do I pray [it is not for their sake only that I make this request], but also for all those who will ever come to believe in [trust in, cling to, rely on] Me through their word and teaching, That they all may be one, [just] as You, Father, are in Me and I in You, that they also may be one in Us, so that the world may believe and be convinced that You have sent Me. I have given to them the glory and honor which You have given Me, that they may be one [even] as We are one: I in them and You in Me, in order that they may become one and perfectly united, that the world may know and [definitely] recognize that You sent Me and that You have loved them [even] as You have loved Me. (John 17:20-23 AB)

God revealed the power of His Word when He revealed to us what it could do when it became a living being. We should allow the Word to germinate in us so we can become the living Word.

And the Word [Christ] became flesh [human, incarnate] and tabernacled [fixed His tent of flesh, lived awhile] among us; and we [actually] saw His glory [His honor, His majesty], such glory as an only begotten son receives from his father, full of grace [favor, loving-kindness] and truth. (John 1:14 AB)

When you are intimately acquainted with God, you delight in obeying His Word even when it is not comfortable.

Why do you call me, "Lord, Lord," and do not do what I say? I will show you what he is like who comes to me and hears my words and puts them into practice. He is like a man building a house that dug down deep and laid the foundation on rock. When a flood came, the torrent struck that house but could not shake it, because it was well built. But the one who hears my words and does not put them into practice is like a man who built a house on the ground without a foundation. The moment the torrent struck that house, it collapsed and its destruction was complete. (Luke 6:46-49 NIV)

There is more of the Lord than we are experiencing now. As we study the Word of God, it will become easy for us to cry out for more revelation of who He is. Our main goal when we come before God should be to know Him. Our hearts' cry should be "Abba, Father."

God wants us to be more like Him and less like the world. The more time we spend in His Word and obeying what it commands, the more we will look like Him. Reproduction comes from the same gene pool, and we have Christ's genes in us through His blood. God's arms are always reaching out to receive us, and His hand is always available to lift us from where we are to where we need to be. God is not hiding from us; He is waiting for us to decrease so He may increase in us.

God's Word should be new and exciting to us each time we pick it up. We should constantly receive fresh revelation from the Holy Spirit. We must never become satisfied with our relationships with the Word of God. The more time we spend studying it, the more we will see there is more to life than material things. Jesus said,

Watch out! Be on your guard against all kinds of greed, a man's life does not consist in the abundance of his possessions. (Luke 12:15 NIV)

I tell you the truth, unless a kernel of wheat falls to the ground and dies it remains only a single seed. But if it dies it produces many seeds. The man who loves his life will lose it, while the man who hates his life in this world will keep it for eternal life. (John 12:24 NIV)

Until we come to the point that it is no longer our will but God's will being done in and through us, He will remain a stranger within.

Jesus knew His purpose; He knew it would cost Him His life. His first prayer in the garden of Gethsemane was, "My Father, if it is possible, may this cup be taken from me. Yet not as I will, but as you will."(Matthew 26:39)

Regardless of what we want, like, or perceive, we are aliens, strangers on earth (1 Peter 2:11). God sent each of us here to fulfill a specific purpose, and we need to go humbly to our Creator to discover our unique purposes. When He reveals our purposes, we may not perceive the calling, but our trust should be in Him. I remember God told me that He called me to be a prophet; I was so scared that I said, "No thank you." Can you imagine the created telling the Creator He had made a mistake? I have studied the Word and prayed all my Christian life. People would tell me I had a call on my life. I didn't understand what that meant, so I refused to embrace that word spoken through them. God, however, was and is gracious; He did not give up on me. He asked me again to be His oracle. I finally said yes to God even though I didn't understand what it meant to be a prophet. God, however, knows our purposes, so we must agree with Him, pursue Him, and embrace what He has called us to do.

## WORSHIP THROUGH PRAISE AND DANCE: FIVE KEYS

The Pentateuch offers a graphic picture of how Moses and the Israelites sang: "I will sing to the Lord, for he is highly exalted.

The horse and its rider he has hurled into the sea" (Exodus 15:1 NIV). Moses' sister, Miriam, took a tambourine and led all the women in a dance: "Then Miriam the prophetess, Aaron's sister, took a tambourine in her hand, and all the women followed her with tambourines and dancing" (Exodus 15:20 NIV).

Psalm 8 contains keys to God's glory and man's dominion: "Lord, our Lord, how majestic is your name in all the earth! You have set your glory in the heavens. Through the praise of children and infants you have established a stronghold against your enemies, to silence the foe and the avenger" (Psalm 8:1-2 NIV).

The first key is to start with praise and adoration of God. Notice here that it is not *my* Lord but *our* Lord; this is us, the corporate body, coming together and acknowledging God's name as majestic. We are saying how sovereign, powerful, royal, great, and splendid is His name.

The first thing God did was to set His praise, worshipful thanksgiving, and honor in the heavens. All creation is full of His glory and is radiant with the excellency of His power. God's goodness and wisdom are manifested everywhere we go. No words can express God's excellency adequately. His name, Jehovah, is excellent. We should glorify Him and show Him what He is worth, praise Him for who He is, and praise Him for where we are right now. Praise is not a bargaining tool. Often, some will say, "I'll praise you so you can bless me." Praise is a weapon that will silence our enemies. "When I consider your heavens, the work of your fingers, the moon and the stars, which you have set in place, what is man that you are mindful of him the son of man that you care for him." (Psalm 8:3-4 NIV).

The second key is meditating on God's Word. To meditate means to reflect or ponder over: "Keep this Book of the Law always on your lips; meditate on it day and night, so that you may be careful to do everything written in it" (Joshua 1:8 NIV). "Yet You have made him but a little lower than God [or heavenly beings], and You have crowned him with glory and honor" (Psalm 8:5 AB).

The third key is knowing who we are and what Christ has done for us. We are joint heirs with Christ. What the first Adam lost, the second Adam restored to us. We are to reign over our circumstances and not let them reign over us. God has given us dominion. We must keep the world under our feet and not let worldly cares and pleasures move us.

> You made him ruler over the works of your hands; you put everything under his feet: all flocks and herds and the beast of the field, the birds of the air and the fish of the sea, all that swim the paths of the seas. (Psalm 8:6-8 NIV)

The fourth key is receiving our inheritance. God has magnified us in creation so we would be lords over the fish of the sea, the beasts of the field, and the fowl of the air. We were created in God's image. To inherit means to receive genetic qualities by transmission from parents to their offspring. Dominion is our divine right.

"Everyone who has left houses or brothers or sisters or father or mother or children or fields for my sake will receive a hundred times as much and will inherit eternal life" (Matthew 19:29 NIV). We don't lose with God; we win. "O Lord, our Lord, how excellent [majestic and glorious] is Your name in all the earth!" (Psalm 8:9 AB).

The fifth key is ending with praise and adoration. The psalmist ends Psalm 8 with adoration and praise to God so we would know how important it is for us to magnify God's name. When we submit to and obey God's Word, we will see His glory and enjoy the sweetness of His name in every situation.

Song and dance have been a form of worship from days of old, and I once received a prophetic song while I was in prayer.

> Burn in me, oh Lord, like in Jeremiah. O God, you are that fire; will you burn in me? I can prophesy because the word burns in me. There is a fire of God, and it is in me; I cannot help but prophesy. Burn in me, oh Lord. Burn in me, oh Lord; go ahead and burn in me. Do not quench that fire, Lord, because it burns in me. I will walk with you; I will dwell in your presence, Lord, where I belong. I belong in that fire; I belong in your fire. The fire of the Lord consumes me. The fire of the Lord is in my bones, and it burns deep within my bones. The fire of the Lord is all over me, who can't help but prophesy.

God continually gives us new songs as we stay in His presence. All we have to do is worship Him in spirit and truth.

## Worship through Silence

According to some, silence is the highest form of worship, surpassing personal supplications, thanksgiving, and praise. When we direct our hearts to God and utter no words of petition, our prayers are pure and humble. We do not suggest to God what He is to do, nor do we indulge in excessive praise and thanksgiving, which inevitably fall short of God's greatness and loving-kindness. This is our ideal approach to God.

## Worship through Thanksgiving and Praise

Thanksgiving and praise are expressions of gratitude for God's manifold blessings: "Give thanks to the Lord, for He is good; His love endures forever" (Psalm 118:1 NIV).

Closely connected to gratitude is the desire to offer praises not as a means of pleasing God but as a means of expressing our gratitude for His daily wonders and miracles. God is exalted above all blessings and praise. "And the Levites—Jeshua, Kadmiel, Bani, Hashabneiah, Sherebiah, Hodiah, Shebaniah and Pethahiah—said: 'Stand up and praise the Lord your God, who is from everlasting to everlasting'" (Nehemiah 9:5 NIV).

I learned to sing and praise the Lord at Bible class. We received a list of songs to sing at home, and my hunger for the Lord caused my daughter and me to sing those songs every day. Even though I was experiencing God in praise, however, I was not satisfied. Some ladies in the Bible study class were going to the park to praise God at 5:30 in the morning. I asked if I could join them, and they said yes. While we were at the park, I asked the Holy Spirit to teach me how to praise and worship God the way He deserved to be honored. I felt so free at the park. A light engulfed me, and I danced and praised God as King David did. Now I am able to enter into praise, worship, and dance anywhere at any time. Praise has become a lifestyle for me. I no longer fear man; I praise God with every ounce of my being.

## Prophetic Song Given to Me while Praising God

I am in God's army, trampling down the forces of darkness. I come into His holy presence, and I magnify His name. I come into your presence, Lord, as a solider, as a mighty solider in your army. I bow before your throne and I say, "Rejuvenate me, strengthen me before I go into battle again. I need your strength, Lord, to carry out your task.

The task you have laid before me is an easy one, Lord, but I must do it in your strength, for I trust in thee, oh God, I do. My Lord, now I come before thee and I say, "Strengthen me that I might go back into the battlefield and subdue your enemy." I am a willing vessel, Lord, and I desire to do thy will. My purpose, Lord, is to destroy the works of the enemy, and I am well able to do it in Christ, for in you I have strength to subdue, in you I have power to overcome.

My Lord, I praise your holy name. Hallelujah to the King of kings! Hallelujah to the Lord of lords! Lord, I praise your holy name; I glorify thee, my Lord. I honor thee, my Lord, in spirit and truth; I praise His majesty who rides upon the horse that was made for Him. He sits tall in the saddle as He marches forth to inspect His troops. He says, "Lie down and rest and let me renew you."

Those who know their God will praise Him in song and dance because God is worthy of praise. It is easy to praise someone you love. If you are not praising God in spirit and truth, He is still a stranger within. To know Him is to praise and worship Him.

# CHAPTER 8

# INTIMACY THROUGH BROKENNESS

*Those who know their God will seek Him through
the intimacy of brokenness.*

You do not delight in sacrifice, or I would bring it; you do not
take pleasure in burnt offerings. The sacrifices of God are
a broken spirit; a broken and contrite heart,
O God, you will not despise.
(Psalm 51:16-17 NIV)

A broken and contrite spirit is a heart totally in subjection
to the Spirit of God, expressing regretful, sorrowful
repentance for sins or offenses. The heart is made up of
the spirit and soul.

For the word of God is quick, and powerful and sharper
than any two edged sword, piercing even to the dividing
asunder of soul and spirit, and of the joints and marrow,
and a discerner of the thoughts and intents of the heart.
(Hebrews 4:12 NIV)

**Spirit (*pneuma*):** This is the real you, the place where new birth takes place, the spiritual Holiest of Holies.

**Soul (*psyche*):** This is not the real you; this is the seat of personality, mind, will, and emotions, the way you are in temperament, characteristics, and traits, the way you think and operate.

> My son, attend to my words; incline thine ear unto my sayings. Let them not depart from thine eyes; keep them in the midst of thine heart. For they are life unto those that find them, and health to all their flesh. Keep thy heart with all diligence; for out of it are the issues of life. (Proverbs 4:20-23 KJV)

*Keep* in this verse means to preserve or protect. Why do we need to keep our hearts? Anytime our affections, passions, and desires are divided, we lose the potential to release the life that comes out of our hearts to change things. Only the Word can divide the spirit and soul and reveal our core. When our hearts are divided, we will have dual interests, desires, and affections. Religious tradition tries to change our behavior and attitudes without changing our nature, and religion changes only conduct, not nature.

Within Christians' spirits is the power of God to bring healing and deliverance. It doesn't matter what circumstances they face; this power within can alter and change them.

A divided heart hinders the flow of God's life (*zoe*) in you. God's life is the only force that will change behavior. If you're wondering why zoe is not flowing from you, check your heart.

> If any of you lacks wisdom, let him ask of God, that giveth to all men liberally, and upbraideth not; and it

shall be given him. But let him ask in faith, nothing wavering; For he that wavereth is like a wave of the sea driven with the wind and tossed. For let not that man think that he shall receive anything of the Lord. A double-minded man is unstable in all his ways. (James 1:5-8 KJV)

The term *double-minded* in the Greek means twice-soulish, a split personality, a divided heart. A divided heart occurs when our spirits reach out in faith but our souls reach out in unbelief, when our spirits' affections are on things above but our soulish affections are on things of the earth.

A new heart also will I give you, and a new spirit will I put within you: and I will take away the stony heart out of your flesh and I will give you a heart of flesh. And I will put my spirit within you and cause you to walk in my statutes, and ye shall keep my judgments and do them. (Ezekiel 36:26-27 KJV)

There are two "hearts" in this passage. Stony hearts are those in the soulish realm, the domain of mind, will, and emotions. This realm contains our behaviors or personalities and are prideful, hard, rebellious, self-willed, arrogant, boastful, and unmanageable.

Hearts of flesh are in the spirit realm. When we are born again, our spirits are immediately saved and our hearts become flexible, pliable, sensitive, gentle, easy to work with, and under control.

The life of God is in the spirit, but it will not be manifest unless it passes through the soul. The spirit man desires the things of God, while the soul seeks to preserve itself and to desire the things of the world. Our struggle begins here. God wants to bring union through the process of agreement. "Can two walk together, except they be agreed?" (Amos 3:3 KJV).

Jesus is our example of a united heart. His spirit and soul were so harmonized that He constantly released the zoe life of God. Everywhere He went, the sick were healed, the dead were raised, devils were cast out, and lepers were cleansed. He spoke words of wisdom and knowledge and met every need presented to Him by releasing zoe. Out of His united heart came the forces of life. Our hearts should be as unified as Jesus' was so the life-giving force of God will flow out of us and change every situation we encounter.

God works in our lives through division and brokenness. During the division stage, God's Word, being quick and powerful, separates the spirit and soul for clarification so we can recognize the difference between our spirits and our souls. God cannot accomplish much through any of us who have not allowed the Word to make that distinction, those of us who want to be strong in their own intellects, natural abilities, and talents.

Brokenness is the tempering and taming of the soul so that it is no longer hard but pliable and flexible. It will become cooperative, sensitive, and submissive to the Spirit of God. "For thus saith the Lord to the men of Judah and Jerusalem, 'Break up your fallow ground, and sow not among thorns'" (Jeremiah 4:3 KJV). Fallow ground is unplowed ground that has been hardened by exposure to the elements. When our souls continue to be exposed to sin and not the Word of God, they become hardened, rough, not pliable, and unresponsive to the touch of God. God was saying through Jeremiah that He would bring brokenness to the soul to remove its strength. When God brings brokenness to the soul, it becomes pliable, easily entreated, sensitive, and obedient to the Spirit of God.

Don't become offended when God begins to probe your life with the Word and exposes every area of your life that does not line up with the Word. Insecurity, unbelief, intimidation, and hardness of heart stop the life of the spirit. The real you, your spirit, is being held prisoner by the soul. God's attributes of life, light, and love are in your spirit.

Jesus said, "Wherefore, by their fruits ye shall know them" (Matthew 7:20 KJV). There are two kinds of Christians. One kind is restricted and imprisoned. They have received God's life but are not able to function because they are wrapped up in the power of self. These Christians are not able to release God's life to others who are depressed, frustrated, unhappy, defeated, angry, critical, judgmental, backbiting, and full of gossip. Everything that comes out of them is death.

The second kind of Christian has learned to release the life of God through the work of brokenness. These Christians have gotten rid of their hard hearts and have learned to release the life of God. It is for this reason that one of the greatest needs in a Christian's life today is brokenness in the heart. Through such brokenness, the spirit will grow in strength as the soul becomes weaker and more sensitive to God. "Create in me a clean heart, O God; and renew a right spirit within me" (Psalm 51:10 KJV).

Brokenness is not God breaking your will; it's God bringing brokenness to your will so it will become tender and soft, allowing it to be sensitive to the Spirit of God. Are you tamed and obedient to the Spirit of God? "And whosoever shall fall on this stone shall be broken; but on whomsoever it shall fall, it will grind him to powder" Matthew 21:44 KJV).

Brokenness deals with taking away the strength of your will. God will break your will only when you ask for it to be broken or when you fall upon the Rock. When God brings brokenness, you will be able to release the life of the Spirit through a heart of flesh. We need to take a good look at our ground and examine those areas we have not allowed God's Word to break up and make pliable.

What does God want?

> For thus saith the high and lofty One that inhabiteth eternity, whose name is Holy: "I dwell in the high and holy place, with him also that is of a contrite and humble spirit, to revive the spirit of the humble and to revive the heart of the contrite ones." (Isaiah 57:15 KJV)

God is going to work through meek people, the contrite ones who are easily entreated and sensitive, who are not talkative, arrogant, boastful, or opinionated. They are slow to speak, not pushy, but transparent. Their spirits can be touched and can touch others. God is no longer a stranger within them, but a friend.

## CONFESSION

God, in the name of Jesus, take Your mighty hand and work brokenness within me. I want to be broken by the hand of the Master. Take out of me arrogance, haughtiness, and pride. Take out of me my self-willed lifestyle. I repent of living life out of my soul, and I ask You to make me into something that can be broken and distributed to people in need.

# CHAPTER 9

# INTIMACY THROUGH REPENTANCE

*Those who know their God will seek Him through
the intimacy of repentance.*

For in him we live and move and have our being. As some
of your own poets have said, "We are His offspring."
Therefore since we are God's offspring, we should not think
that the divine being is like gold or silver or stone—an image
made by man's design and skill. In the past God
overlooked such ignorance, but now he commands
all people everywhere to repent.
(Acts 17:28-30 NIV)

*R*epent means to have a change of mind in respect to sin, God, and self. This change has to be followed by sorrow. Though sorrow may cause repentance, it is not in itself repentance. Repentance is not just for sinners; it is also for believers. It is not a one-time activity; it is an action God's people are called to do until Jesus returns. Repentance requires a soft, pliable heart that responds to and acts upon godly reproof, is tender, and is easily molded by the Holy Spirit.

Christians who maintain repentant hearts receive God's special attention and will be overtaken with incredible blessings. The number-one characteristic of a repentant heart is a readiness and willingness to acknowledge guilt, to accept blame for wrongdoing. It says, "I am the one, Lord; I have sinned."

If you do not admit your sin, there can be no repentance: "Godly sorrow brings repentance that leads to salvation and leaves no regret" (2 Corinthians 7:10a NIV). If you blame your actions on other people and are not willing to acknowledge you are wrong, you have no need to repent. People should not have that much control over you. You should base your behavior on the Word and not on your circumstances.

> When Pilate saw that he was getting nowhere, but instead an uproar was starting, he took water and washed his hands in front of the crowd. "I am innocent of this man's blood," he said. "It is your responsibility!" (Matthew 27:24 NIV)

Before Pilate turned Jesus over to the Roman soliders, he wanted the world to know that whatever happened to Jesus wasn't his fault. He asked for a basin of water, dipped his hands in it, and absolved himself before the angry mob; he declared himself innocent of Christ's blood.

Pilate's hands were not clean, however; he handed the Son of God over to murderers, and that kind of thinking shuts a person off from any possibility of repentance. Pilate believed he did nothing wrong because he had washed his hands of everything. If a prophet would have told him, "You need to repent," Pilate would have said, "Why should I repent? I have done no wrong."

When people slander another in our presence and we come into agreement with them, we are just as guilty because we agreed with the slanderers. "If we claim to be without sin, we deceive ourselves, and the truth is not in us" (1 John 1:8 NIV). "If we claim we have not sinned, we make him out to be a liar and his word has no place in our lives" (1 John 1:10 NIV). Repentance brings freedom. We need to admit we have sinned, be dealt with, and ask for forgiveness.

Malachi was a prophet sent by God to reprove Israel. Each time he went to the people with a strong message, however, they reacted with counterfeit innocence. The first time Malachi came to them, he preached, You have profaned the holiness of the Lord. (Malachi chapter1) the people were shocked and wanted to know what they had done wrong. They knew how to weep and cover the altar with tears. God rejected all their sacrifices because of their sin. They were divorcing their wives and marrying heathen women after God told them not to. Malachi asked, "You ask, Why? It is because the Lord is acting as the witness between you and the wife of your youth, because you have broken faith with her though she is your partner, the wife of your marriage covenant" (Malachi 2:14 NIV).

Their hearts were full of sin while they continued going to the altar, performing all their religious activities. They openly rebelled against God's commands. They denied their sins to themselves because they believed they were clean.

The second time Malachi came to them, he said, "Ye have wearied the Lord with your words" (Malachi 2:17a KJV). They were saying things that shocked God; their profanities wearied God. The people responded in counterfeit innocence again, however: "Wherein have we wearied him? When ye say, Every one that doeth evil is good in the sight of the Lord, and he delighted in them; or, Where is the God of judgment?" (Malachi 2:17 b, c KJV).

The people were encouraging evildoers in the congregation; they knew these rebels were in sin, but they assured them that all was well and that no judgment would fall on them. They were calling evil good, and good evil. Those who embrace sin cause curses to come upon them.

"Again, Malachi came to them, crying, 'You have robbed God!' but the people asked, 'What do you mean? How have we robbed God?' 'In tithes and offerings'" (Malachi 3:8b KJV). They were robbing God of their best by bringing garbage—injured, diseased, lame, and blind animals—to the Lord's altar.

Finally, Malachi gave up preaching to them because they would not hear him. In the final chapter of his book, he went to a small, discerning, and repentant remnant. These people received his reproof; their hearts were moved by the Spirit of God, and they were blessed mightily.

I'm going to share with you four benefits available to us if you repent. The first benefit of repentance is a new and clearer vision of Jesus Christ. Daniel received a revelation from God, but he had no understanding, so he repented, fasted, and prayed. Look what happened after Daniel repented for himself and God's people who were rebellious, wicked, disobedient, and not listening to the prophets.

> I looked up and there before me was a man dressed in linen, with a belt of the finest gold around his waist. His body was like chrysolite, his face like lightning, his eyes like flaming torches, his arms and legs like the gleam of burnished bronze, and his voice like the sound of a multitude. I, Daniel, was the only one who saw the vision; the men with me did not see it, but such terror

overwhelmed them that they fled and hid themselves.
(Daniel 10:5-7 NIV)

After Daniel repented, the Holy Spirit open Daniel's eyes and gave
him a clear vision of Christ in all His glory. None of his friends saw
the vision; Jesus walks among only the truly repentant hearts that
do not hide from Him.

The second benefit of repentance is the removal of all fear. If
you acknowledge your sins, showing godly sorrow, you can look
confidently into the Master's face. You will not quake with fear when
you hear a word of reproof. You'll stand before Christ's flaming eyes
while everyone else is fleeing!

> A hand touched me and set me trembling on my
> hands and knees. He said, "Daniel, you who are highly
> esteemed, consider carefully the words I am about to
> speak to you, and stand up, for I have now been sent to
> you." And when he said this to me, I stood up trembling.
> Then he continued, "Do not be afraid, Daniel. Since the
> first day that you set your mind to gain understanding
> and to humble yourself before your God, your words
> were heard, and I have come in response to them."
> (Daniel 10:10-12 NIV)

When Christians hide their sin, they do not prosper. Unrepentant
hearts are full of fear and restlessness, while repentant hearts walk
each day without any trace of fear. God's hand plucks fear from the
root and blesses repentant hearts with His divine favor.

The third benefit of repentance is a new pair of lips: "Then one who
looked like a man touched my lips and I opened my mouth and
began to speak" (Daniel 10:16a NIV). When Daniel spoke, he spoke

as unto the Lord. When the prophet Isaiah stood before the Lord in all His holiness, He said, "I am a man of unclean lips" (Isaiah 6:5 NIV). God took the coals of fire from the altar, put the tongs on Isaiah's lips, and burned out all dross, self, and flesh—everything that was not like Him. He gave Isaiah a new pair of lips. God does this for every person who repents! Once your lips have been purged, the words that flow from you will be pure.

The fourth benefit of repentance is peace and strength: "'Do not be afraid, O man highly esteemed,' he said. 'Peace! Be strong now; be strong.' When he spoke to me, I was strengthened and said, 'Speak, my Lord, since you have given me strength'" (Daniel 10:19 NIV). Daniel had been mourning for sin, praying, fasting, and weeping; as a result, he was totally drained. Jesus touched his body and flooded him with peace and strength. Similarly, repentant Christians can be downcast, totally wiped out, and overwhelmed by sorrow and weariness, but the Lord will always come to touch their bodies and give them renewed peace and strength.

Do you have a repentant heart? Or should I ask, do you want one? Let God search and examine your heart. Ask the Holy Spirit to reveal everything you have said or done that grieved Him, wait until He reveals those areas, and repent. If you have slandered or gossiped about someone, admit it, repent, and go on. I promise you that if you make all things right, God's favor will be released in your life to a degree you have yet to experience. God will open up your eyes, ears, and understanding, and you will be given a revelation of things to come. "Blessed be the Lord, who daily loadeth us with benefits, even the God of our salvation" (Psalm 68:19 KJV).

Christians who live repented lifestyles will become intimately acquainted with God. He is no longer a stranger within because they know the joy of a repentant life.

# CHAPTER 10

# INTIMACY THROUGH JUSTIFICATION

*Those who know their God will seek Him through
the intimacy of justification.*

He was delivered over to death for our sins and was
raised to life for our justification.
(Romans 4:25 NIV)

Justification is a judicial act of God by which sinners are
declared innocent as if they had never sinned, not because
of works, but because of Christ's righteousness; justification
is apprehended by faith, according to *Smith's Bible Dictionary*.
Justification is not the act of *making* someone righteous, but the
act of *declaring* someone righteous, according to the *Greek and
Hebrew Study Bible*. Justification is to render just or innocent, free,
justified, righteous, acquitted (for Christ's sake), according to *Strong's
Exhaustive Concordance of the Bible* 1347, *Dikaiosis*.

Christ died to make atonement for our sins. His death and
resurrection paid our bill in full.

> He was pierced for our transgressions, He was crushed
> for our iniquities; the punishment that brought us peace
> was upon Him, and by His wounds we are healed. We
> all, like sheep, have gone astray, each of us has turned to
> his own way; and the Lord has laid on Him the iniquity
> of us all. (Isaiah 53:5-6 NIV)

Jesus Christ offered the acceptable sacrifice for all sin. He came
once and for all and at just the right time to take away all sin by
sacrificing himself.

> Christ demonstrates His own love for us in this: While
> we were still sinners, Christ died for us. Since we have
> now been justified by his blood, how much more shall
> we be saved from God's wrath through Him! (Romans
> 5:8-9 NIV)

We were God's enemies, but He made us friends through the death
of His Son: "For if, when we were God's enemies, we were reconciled
to Him through the death of His Son, how much more, having been
reconciled, shall we be saved through His life!" (Romans 5:10 NIV).

By trusting in Jesus' sacrifice, we are freed from the separation and
penalty of sin: "For we know that our old self was crucified with Him
so that the body of sin might be done away with, that we should no
longer be slaves to sin" (Romans 6:6 NIV).

We know our old life died with Christ on the cross so our sinful
selves would have no power over us and we would not be slaves to
sin. We are not justified by our works but by our dependence on the
love and righteousness of Christ. We can never expect to receive our
inheritance by the law. The first covenant was unsure, but now, by
faith, we receive God's grace and are accepted by Christ.

All who rely on observing the law are under a curse, for it is written: "Cursed is everyone who does not continue to do everything written in the Book of the Law." Clearly no one is justified before God by the law, because "The righteous will live by faith." The law is not based on faith; on the contrary, "The man who does these things will live by them." Christ redeemed us from the curse of the law by becoming a curse for us, for it is written: "Cursed is everyone who is hung on a tree." He redeemed us in order that the blessing given to Abraham might come to the Gentiles through Christ Jesus, so that by faith we might receive the promise of the Spirit. (Galatians 3:10-14 NIV)

The promise God gives us is not based on something we did or will do; rather, it is based on His grace through faith, which we enter into when we believe in Him. If God's promise were received by works, that would eliminate our personal trust in Him and turn our holy promises into business deals, which would mean we would have a contract we would never be able to collect on. God's promises cannot be broken; their fulfillment depends entirely on trusting and embracing Him and His ways. "For it is by grace you have been saved, through faith and this not from yourselves; it is the gift of God—not by works, so that no one can boast" (Ephesians 2:8-9 NIV).

God's promise is a pure gift (in Greek, *charisma*, an undeserved benefit that is a result of grace). The only way we can get in on it is to receive it by faith. God justly treats as righteous those who believe in Jesus Christ. Justified believers walk in Christ's righteousness, and nothing is laid to their charge.

To be intimate with God, we must know the facts of our union and identification with Christ's death and resurrection. We must also receive the atoning work of Christ, which gives us access to our holy Father. God wants us near Him at all times so He will no longer be a stranger within.

## CONFESSION

Justification has freed me; I know my inheritance cannot be received by the law or works but only by faith in Jesus Christ and His atoning blood. The first covenant was not sure, but by faith I have received God's grace. I am as though I had never sinned (Acts 13:39).

# CHAPTER 11

## INTIMACY THROUGH COMMUNION

*Those who know their God will seek Him through the*
*intimacy of the Lord's Supper/Communion.*

While they were eating, Jesus took bread, gave thanks and
broke it, and gave it to His disciples, saying, "Take and eat;
this is my body." Then He took the cup, gave thanks
and offered it to them, saying, "Drink from it, all of you. This is
my blood of the covenant, which is poured out for
many for the forgiveness of sins."
(Matthew 26:26-28 NIV)

*T*ake is a command or order to grab as one's own. *Drink* is to
accept without question. *Forgiveness* is to send off or away or
to separate sin from the sinner. Jesus commands us to accept
without question that He has separated us from our sins and that
we are no longer slaves to sin.

In the Old Testament, meals were never simply about eating food
and quenching thirst; they were about strengthening the social
bonds of kinship, friendship, and fellowship and ways of enjoying

God's presence and provisions. God's people expected His presence at ordinary meals.

The Lord's Supper, also known as Communion, replaced the Passover feast. During Passover, the bread and wine were memorials of deliverance from Egypt. Today, they are memorials of what our Lord and Master did for us. His body was broken and His blood was shed for the remission of our sins.

> For I received from the Lord Himself that I passed on to you [it was given to me personally], that the Lord Jesus on the night when He was treacherously delivered up and while His betrayal was in progress took bread, and when He had given thanks, He broke it and said, "Take, eat. This is my body, which is broken for you. Do this to call me [affectionately] to remembrance." (1 Corinthians 11:23-24 AB)

> For the Bread of God is He who comes down out of heaven and gives life to the world. They said to Him, "Lord, give us this bread always [all the time]!" Jesus replied, "I am the Bread of Life. He who comes to me will never be hungry, and he who believes in and cleaves to and trusts in and relies on me will never thirst any more [at any time]." (John 6:33-35 AB)

> And their sins and iniquities will I remember no more. Now where remission of these is, there is no more offering for sin. (Hebrews 10:17-18 KJV)

In the Old Testament, the sacrifices were types and shadows of atonement for sins that pointed to Christ and were fulfilled in Him. Jesus shed His blood for the forgiveness of sin once and for all. Sin interrupts our fellowship with the Lord, but upon our confession of sin, we attain divine forgiveness.

Jesus is the bread of life who gives us support, endurance, and strength. He transfuses something dead—us—with new or renewed life.

> Similarly when supper was ended, He took the cup also, saying, "This cup is the new covenant [ratified and established] in My blood. Do this as often as you drink [it], to call me [affectionately] to remembrance. For every time you eat this bread and drink this cup you are representing and signifying and proclaiming the fact of the Lord's death until He comes [again]." (1 Corinthians 11:25-26 AB)

- cup—suffering or affliction
- new covenant—a binding agreement or contract
- drink—to accept without question
- eat—to accept what one has fought against, that is, loss of dominion
- death—to give up one's life

Christ is saying the suffering and affliction He was about to go through would ratify and establish the new binding agreement that dominion has been restored to mankind and that we are complete in Him. Every time we eat the bread and drink the wine, we are accepting without question and praising Him publicly for the dominion His life restored to us.

> So then whoever eats the bread or drinks the cup of the Lord in a way that is unworthy [of Him] will be guilty of [profaning and sinning against] the body and blood of the Lord. Let a man [thoroughly] examine

> himself, and [only when he has done] so should he eat
> of the bread and drink of the cup. For anyone who
> eats and drinks without discriminating and recognizing
> with due appreciation that [it is Christ's] body, eats and
> drinks a sentence [a verdict of judgment] upon himself.
> (1 Corinthians 11:27-29 AB)

Those of us who are lacking in excellence must carefully look into our states to see if we are joined in love to Christ and to each member of the body. Our sins have been atoned for; however, every work must come into judgment. The result is reward or loss of the reward.

The Lord's Supper, Communion, looks back in time to proclaim Jesus' death and forward to the end of time. By sharing Communion, believers proclaim hope and trust that they will share a meal with Jesus.

Communion is for Jesus Christ and His friends who understand Him to be Lord, who remember God's faithful provisions for His people through salvation, and who are sealed by the blood of the New Covenant.

Those who know Christ will pick up their crosses and die daily to their selves. They will be thankful to God for the body and blood of His Son. They will receive in meekness everything that Christ has done, they will look in the mirror and see Jesus, and they will also see Jesus in other members of the body of Christ.

The Lord loves diversity; that is why He made us all unique. We should all love diversity in the body of Christ; however, we need to respect order and purpose. We should also expect to learn something new and creative from diverse members. Those of us who know the Creator and are becoming like Him should be creative by using the gifts God has given us such as serving, encouraging and contributing to the needs of other.

We must all discern the Lord's body to fully appreciate who Christ is. There is no big "I" and little "you"; we are all one in Christ. When we learn to discern and appreciate the body of Christ, He will no longer be a stranger within.

# CHAPTER 12

# INTIMACY THROUGH HUMILITY

*Those who know their God will seek Him through
the intimacy of humility.*

Be still and know that I am God; I will be exalted among the
nations, I will be exalted in the earth.
(Psalm 46:10 NIV)

My heart is not proud, O Lord, my eyes are not haughty; I do
not concern myself with great matters or things too wonderful
for me. But I have stilled and quieted my soul; like a weaned
child with its mother, like a weaned child is my soul within me.
(Psalm 131:1-2 NIV)

Our road to intimacy begins with humility and sanctification.
We are continually being weaned from the world and sin.
To accomplish God's purposes for us, we have to give
ourselves to Him. Weaning ourselves from sin, from the world, is a
daily process. We go from sin to holiness, from the world to Christ,
from self to God. A quiet soul is sweet and powerful. To quiet the
soul is a difficult task, but a calm soul knows and appreciates God,
who speaks in a still, small, quiet voice.

Most Christians are too busy or agitated to know His voice, but busyness is just an excuse, and excuses are the crutches of the uncommitted. How can we say we love God if we do not spend time with Him in solitude? Our souls have to be quiet so we can hear Him speak.

"Pride goes before destruction, a haughty spirit before a fall. Better to be lowly in spirit and among the oppressed than to share plunder with the proud" (Proverbs 16:18-19 NIV). What is pride? Exaltation of oneself; having no room for God; or refusal to obey, depend on, or worship God. Pride is worship of oneself, other people, or the world. "In his pride the wicked does not seek Him; in all his thoughts there is no room for God" (Psalm 10:4 NIV).

Some people are so proud that there is no room for God in their thoughts. They deny that God has a right to run their lives. Pride will destroy them.

> How you have fallen from heaven, O morning star, son of dawn! You have been cast down to the earth, you who once laid low the nations! You said in your heart, "I will" ascend to heaven; "I will" raise my throne above the stars of God; "I will" sit enthroned on the mount of assembly, on the utmost heights of the sacred mountain. "I will" ascend above the tops of the clouds; "I will" make myself like the Most High. (Isaiah 14:12-14 NIV)

Satan was full of himself and decided he did not need God because he considered himself God's equal. He forgot that God had created him and that all he possessed came from God.

In the Daniel 4, we read that Nebuchadnezzar was troubled because he had a dream about an enormous tree in the middle of the land.

It was strong, and its top touched the sky; it was visible to the ends of the earth. Its leaves were beautiful, and its fruit was abundant. Under it, the beasts of the field found shelter, and the birds of the air lived in its branches. Nebuchadnezzar saw a holy messenger come down from heaven saying,

> Cut down the tree and trim its branches, strip off its leaves, scatter its fruit, let the animals flee from under it and the birds from its branches. But let the stump and its roots bound with iron and bronze remain in the ground in the grass of the field. Let him be drench with the dew of heaven and let him be given the mind of an animal, till seven years pass. The verdict was rendered so that the living may know that the Most High is sovereign over the kingdoms of men and gives them to anyone he wishes and sets over them the lowliest of men. (Daniel 4:14-17 NIV)

The king was so troubled that he called the wise men of Babylon to interpret the dream, but none of them could. Daniel came before him, but before Daniel spoke, the king said, "The spirit of the holy gods is in him and no mystery is too difficult for him." The king acknowledged Daniel's ability and gave credit to God.

Daniel told Nebuchadnezzar that he wished the dream had applied to his enemies but that it did not; it applied to him. The Most High would drive the king away from the people, and he would live with the animals, eat grass as cattle do, and be drenched with the dew of heaven for seven years until he acknowledged that the Most High was sovereign over the kingdoms of men and could give them to anyone He wished.

The command to leave the stump and its roots meant that Nebuchadnezzar's kingdom would be restored when he acknowledged that heaven ruled. Daniel advised him to repent of his sins by doing what was right and to repent of his wickedness by being kind to the oppressed. Afterward, God might permit his prosperity to continue. God always gives us space to repent.

The king, however, did not listen to Daniel. One year later, he was walking on the roof of his palace in Babylon, asking, "Is this the great Babylon I have built as the royal residence, by my mighty power and for the glory of my majesty?" (Daniel 4:29-30 NIV). The words were still on his lips when a voice from heaven said, "Your royal authority has been taken away from you." Immediately what had been said about him was fulfilled. His body was drenched with the dew of heaven until his hair grew like the feathers of an eagle and his nails like the claws of a bird. He became too proud, so God disposed of him. God won't share His glory with anyone.

God is so merciful, however. At the end of seven years, Nebuchadnezzar raised his eyes toward heaven, and his sanity was restored. He praised and glorified the Most High, who lives forever. He said,

> God's dominion is an eternal dominion; His kingdom endures from generation to generation. All the peoples of the earth are regarded as nothing. He does as he pleases with the powers of heaven and the peoples of the earth. No one can hold back his hand or say to him: "What have you done?" (Daniel 4:34-35 NIV)

Nebuchadnezzar finally understood that God was the God of gods and the King of kings. His sanity, honor, and splendor were restored. His advisors and noblemen came looking for him. He once again ascended his throne and became even greater than before.

Isaiah 2 talks about the necessity of humility in the day of the Lord.

"The eyes of the arrogant man will be humbled and the pride of men brought low; The Almighty has a day in store for all the proud and lofty, for all that is exalted [and they will be humbled]" (Isaiah 2:11-12 NIV). "The arrogance of man will be brought low and the pride of men humbled; the Lord alone will be exalted in that day, and the idols will totally disappear" (Isaiah 2:17-18 NIV).

Humility is the quality or state of being humble, not proud or haughty, not arrogant or assertive, but lacking all signs of pride. Proud people will be made humble, and they will bow with shame.

> Let not the wise man boast of his wisdom or the strong man boast of his strength or the rich man boast of his riches, but let him who boasts boast about this: that he understands and knows me, that I am the Lord who exercises kindness, justice and righteousness on earth, for in these I delight, declares the Lord. (Jeremiah 9:23-24 NIV)

To avoid being prideful, we must recognize who we are and who God is. God, our creator and sustainer, is worthy of our worship and praise. We must be humble enough to acknowledge our total reliance on His grace. If we do not, we will be proud but His enemy. God is a loving Father who delights to provide for His children who call upon Him in humility. It is impossible to walk in pride when we really know God. Being in His presence makes us realize how great He is and how small we are. As a result, our hearts will become humble and grateful.

God knows those who are His, and everyone who confesses the name of the Lord must turn away from wickedness. Pride is wickedness in the sight of God. Those of us who know Him will walk in humility; those of us who continue to walk in pride will not know Him; He will be a stranger within.

# CHAPTER 13

# ORDER AND AUTHORITY

*Those who know their God will seek Him through
order and authority.*

Everyone must submit himself to the governing authorities, for
there is no authority except that which God has established.
The authorities that exist have been established by God.
Consequently, he who rebels against the authority is rebelling
against what God has instituted, and those who do so will
bring judgment on themselves.
(Romans 13:1-2 NIV)

There are two principles in the universe: God's authority
and Satan's rebelliousness. God's authority is God Himself,
and He institutes all authority on earth. God upholds all
things by the powerful word of His authority. Those of us who desire
intimacy with God must know the authority of God. There are two
important matters in the universe: trusting God's salvation and
obeying God's authority.

All kingdom authority and glory belong to God alone. We preach
the gospel to bring people under God's authority, but if we have not
met God's authority, how can we deal with Satan?

Paul persecuted the church until he met authority in the form of Jesus. After that, he immediately acknowledged Him as Lord. God uses His power to maintain His authority, which is the greatest force we will ever come up against. If we do not know God's authority, we will not submit to His delegated authority. "Does the Lord delight in burnt offerings and sacrifices as much as in obeying the voice of the Lord? To obey is better than the fat of rams" (1 Samuel 15:22 NIV). Obedience is better than sacrifice. Before authority is expressed, there must be subjection. "For rebellion is like the sin of divination, and arrogance like the evil of idolatry" (1 Samuel 15:23 NIV).

Our relationship with God is regulated by whether we submit to His authority. Saul did not respect God's authority or Samuel, God's delegated authority. When God gave Adam His Word, He placed him in authority. Eve was under Adam's authority. Eve was deceived, but both she and Adam transgressed; they disobeyed God's authority, which caused the fall of mankind (Genesis 2:16-17). Satan's assault in the garden was threefold: he introduced doubt, unbelief, and the denial of God's Word. Satan made Eve believe God was keeping something from her, and Eve accepted Satan's word, which caused her to sin against God's authority. Satan can't make us do anything; we have to agree with his thought and then act on it (Genesis 3:1-6).

Aaron was the high priest, which made him God's delegated authority. His sons were his helpers. His sons decided to offer a sacrifice without Aaron being present. They saw him sacrifice many times, so they knew how to do it. However, they forgot about God's order and to whom He had delegated His authority. Since they sacrificed apart from Aaron, they worked independently of God, which is self-imposed worship or "strange fire" (Leviticus 10:1-2). "Strange fire" refers to serving without an order, assuming authority that does not belong to you, or serving without obedience to authority.

I remember when a visiting minister came to my former church and the pastor gave him the order he should follow in the service. However, that minister changed the order of service to suit himself. As he began to preach, I heard the words "strange fire." I did not understand what that meant, but I knew something was wrong. Later, the pastor said that the minister had taken unauthorized liberty in some areas of the service.

In Numbers 12, when Miriam and Aaron spoke against Moses because he had married a black woman, God heard their words and judged them accordingly. We are never to despise God's chosen vessels, the ones to whom He gives His authority.

We should fear speaking against God's delegated authority because that is speaking against God. The issue is not whether we can do what those in authority are doing—it's that God has not given us the authority to do so. God desires the church to give Him absolute preeminence (superiority) so His authority may prevail. He also wants us to be obedient to His delegated authority.

> Submit yourselves for the Lord's sake to every authority instituted among men: Whether to the king, as the supreme authority, or to governors, who are sent by him to punish those who do wrong and to commend those who do right. (1 Peter 2: 13-14 NIV)

There are three areas of obedience in these verses:

**In the world:** God is the source of all authority in the universe. All governing authorities are instituted by God and represent His authority. God established this system to represent Him. We must not resist or disobey authority unless what we are requested to do is contrary to the Word of God. It is rebelliousness to carelessly criticize or denounce the government and those who represent it. God will judge all forms of rebellion; insubordination to authority is mutiny against God.

**In the family:** "Wives, submit to your husbands as to the Lord. For the husband is the head of the wife as Christ is the head of the church, his body, of which he is the Savior" (Ephesians 5:22-24 KJV). God has set up His order of authority in the home, but many Christians pay no attention to His order. If they did, many problems in the home would disappear. God set husbands up as the delegated authority of Christ in their homes. If wives do not respect the delegated authority of their husbands, they will not submit to that authority. Women must realize it is a matter of God's order and authority and not a matter of their husbands' superiority.

**In the church:** "The elders who direct the affairs of the church well are worthy of double honor, especially those whose work is preaching and teaching" (1 Timothy 5:17 (NIV). God has an order for His church: Jesus the head, elders, deacons and deaconess, and the ministry of helps. There are also those who labor in the preaching and teaching of God's Word. The church should have two senses: one of sin and one of authority. Delegated authority is designed to replenish our lack, bestow His riches, and supply the needs of the weak; it is not meant to oppress, hurt, or trouble us.

Unless the matter of authority is solved in the church, it will always experience chaos. Those of us who truly know Him will always respect those in authority, a key to intimacy with God. Do you know and respect all authority instituted by God whether you agree with it or not, or is God still a stranger within?

## Confession

Father, I repent of my rebellion to authority. I now recognize that all authority is instituted by God. I humbly submit to those who have rule over me, and I thank You for them.

# CHAPTER 14

# BUILD ME AN ALTAR

Build there an altar to the Lord your God
(Deuteronomy 27:5)

*Those who know their God will build Him an altar.*

An altar is the central point of worship; it is the place on which sacrifices are made to God and where we meet God daily. Where do you meet with God? Have you built him an altar in your heart?

According to *Webster's*, an altar is a structure used as a center of worship. The mercy seat is a love seat; we are that mercy seat on earth. To build an altar before God, we must:

- forsake everything displeasing to God and purify ourselves;
- return to obedience to God's revealed will;
- remember our past blessings; and
- have assurance of our divine protection from all our enemies.

In the Old Testament, there were eight types of offerings that spoke of Christ's nature.

**The drink offering** was always poured out, never drunk. It speaks of Christ's life being poured out for our sins. Jesus said, "I am poured out like water, and all my bones are out of joint. My heart is like wax; it is softened [with anguish] and melted down within me" (Psalm 22:14 NIV). Our lives are to be poured out for the gospel.

**The burnt offering**, a pleasing aroma, was symbolic of Christ's offering of His body without spot or wrinkle to God. The offering had to be acceptable. Today, we must offer our sinless bodies to God as a burnt offering to do His will.

In 1 Leviticus, five creatures are named as acceptable for burnt offerings made to God. A young bull or ox typifies Christ, the patient, enduring servant. Your attitude should be the same as that of Christ Jesus, humble and obedient.

> Who, being in very nature God, did not consider equality with God something to be grasped, but made himself nothing, taking the very nature of a servant, being made in human likeness, and being found in appearance as a man, He humbled Himself and became obedient to death—even death on a cross. (Philippians 2:6-8 NIV)

A *sheep* or *lamb* typifies Christ's unresisting self-surrendering death on the cross. We must take up our cross and follow Him.

> He was oppressed and afflicted, yet He did not open His mouth; He was led like a lamb to the slaughter, and as a sheep before her shearers is silent, so he did not open His mouth. (Isaiah 53:7 NIV)

A *goat* typifies sinners. When used sacrificially, it speaks of Christ being numbered with the transgressors.

> God made Him who had no sin to be sin for us, so that in Him we might become the righteousness of God. (2 Corinthians 5:21 NIV)

When Jesus hung on the cross, He became a curse for us so we would no longer be slaves to sin.

> Christ redeemed us from the curse of the law by becoming a curse for us, for it is written: "Cursed is everyone is hung on a tree." (Galatians 3:13 (NIV)

*Doves* and *pigeons* typify the mourning of innocence. These were the sacrifices of a poor man. Jesus became a poor man's sacrifice.

> If he cannot afford a lamb, he is to bring two doves or two young pigeons to the Lord as a penalty for his sin. (Leviticus 5:7 NIV)

> For you know the grace of our Lord Jesus Christ, that though He was rich, yet for your sakes He became poor, so that you through His poverty might become rich. (2 Corinthians 8:9 NIV)

His pathway to poverty began with His emptying Himself of His pre-incarnate glory, and it ended in us becoming rich.

In each of these six sacrifices, mature Christians who are intimately acquainted with the Lord see a type and shadow of the crucified Christ.

We have to die to ourselves daily so that Christ can live through us to reach a dying world.

**Grain or meal offering** give a pleasing aroma.

> When someone brings a grain offering to the Lord, his
> offering is to be of fine flour. He is to pour oil on it, put
> incense on it and take it to Aaron's sons, the priests.
> The priest shall take a handful of the fine flour and
> oil, together with all the incense, and burn this as a
> memorial portion on the altar, an offering made by fire,
> an aroma pleasing to the Lord. (Leviticus 2:1-2 NIV)

- Fine flour speaks of the evenly balanced character of Christ.
- Fire speaks of His testing and suffering unto death.
- Incense speaks of the fragrance of His life before God.
- Absence of leaven speaks of the truth of His character.
- Absence of honey speaks of no natural sweetness apart from grace.
- The oil mixture speaks of Christ born of the Holy Spirit.
- The oil upon the altar speaks of the baptism of the Holy Spirit.
- The oven speaks of the unseen suffering of Christ—His inner agony.
- The griddle speaks of His evident suffering.
- The salt speaks of the pungency of the truth of God.

All of the above characteristics should be manifest in our lives if we are abiding in the Vine.

**Fellowship or peace offerings** offer a pleasing aroma. In the Old Testament, fellowship offerings were rendered as thanksgiving for divine help and blessing. This peace offering also pictures friendship between God's people and friendship with God.

> If someone's offering is a fellowship offering, and he
> offers an animal from the herd, whether male or female,
> he is to present before the Lord an animal without defect.
> (Leviticus 3:1 NIV)

Christ is made peace (Colossians 1:20), preached peace (Ephesians 2:17), and is our peace (Ephesians 2:14). In Christ, God and sinners meet in peace: sinners are reconciled to God through the blood of Christ and then have fellowship with the Father. The fellowship offering for the priest consisted of the breast (affections) and thighs (strength).

We as priests unto God must be in intimate fellowship with the Father.

> But you are a chosen people, a royal priesthood, a holy
> nation, a people belonging to God, that you may declare
> the praises of him who called you out of darkness into
> his wonderful light. (1 Peter 2:9 NIV)

In exercising the office of priest, New Testament believers are sacrificers who offer a fourfold sacrifice:

- their own bodies (Romans 12:1)
- fruit coming from lips that praise Him continually (Hebrews 13:15)
- their substance, their possessions (Romans 12:13)
- their service, doing good (Hebrews 13:16)

The New Testament believer, as a priest, has access to Christ the High Priest and to God in the Holy of Holies.

**The sin or guilt offering** was not a pleasing aroma but was required for all unintentional sin. It is an offering made by a person who has done something wrong to become right with God. A person who does something wrong must make things right with the person who was wronged.

> If the anointed priest sins, bringing guilt on the people, he must bring to the Lord a young bull without defect as a sin offering for the sins he has committed. (Leviticus 4:3 NIV)

This offering consisted of one young bull for the high priest and one for the congregation. It could also be a male goat for a ruler and a female goat or lamb for the common people.

The sin or guilt offering speaks of Christ's substitutionary and atoning work on Calvary. Christ was made sin for us, setting us free from the law. We are free from the law of sin and death by the blood of Jesus.

**The trespass offering** was not a pleasing aroma but was required for unintentional sin against holy things or a neighbor (Leviticus 5:1-6). It consisted of one ram without defect and restitution of the value of what was taken plus one fifth of the value. Poor persons could bring two doves or pigeons or fine flour. The trespass offering speaks of Christ's substitutionary and atoning work on Calvary. Also known as a penalty or guilt offering, it emphasized the injury caused by sin rather than the guilt.

**The guilt offering** was not a pleasing aroma but was required of anyone who was unfaithful to the Lord or who deceived, stole, cheated, lied, or swore falsely. That person had to make restitution in full and add a fifth of the value to it (Leviticus 6:1-7).

**The burnt offering** was not a pleasing aroma but was required. It consisted of two bullocks, one ram, and seven lambs (Leviticus 6:8-13). It speaks of the complete and total consecration of Christ to doing the Father's will.

By the power of Christ's redeeming blood, all sin, iniquity, transgressions, and uncleanness are fully atoned. He has done it all for us, and all He asks is for us to prepare an altar in our hearts attesting that we will obey Him in every way and live our lives as He did, bringing glory to the Father.

The New Testament uses the language of sacrifices to describe what God wants from Christians. Instead of animal sacrifices, Christians are to give spiritual service to God. God wants a sacrifice from us in the form of living service.

## CONFESSION

I will live a life of love, just as Christ loved me and gave Himself up for me. I am a living stone, being built into a spiritual house to be a holy priesthood, offering spiritual sacrifices acceptable to God through Jesus Christ.

# CHAPTER 15

# BECOMING A SERVANT

*Those who know their God will seek Him through servanthood.*

*The spirit of a servant is foundational to those who
are effective witnesses in the world.*

You know that those who are regarded as rulers of the Gentiles
lord it over them and their high officials exercise authority
over them. Not so with you. Instead whoever wants to be
first must be slave of all. For even the Son of Man did
not come to be served, but to serve, and to
give His life as a ransom for many.
(Mark 10:42-45 NIV)

A servant is one who serves others, one who performs
duties about the person or home of a master or personal
employer.

Two words used in the New Testament more frequently for *serve*,
*servant*, or *serving* are *douleo*, which means to be a slave, to serve,
to obey, or to submit, and *diakoneo*, which means to minister to
someone. This is where we get the word *deacon*.

*Webster's* defines a servant as a slave, one who assists or attends others or supplies services to others.

> Whoever wants to become great among you must be your servant, and whoever wants to be first must be your slave—just as the Son of Man did not come to be served, but to serve, and to give His life as a ransom for many. (Matthew 20:26-28 NIV)

To be a servant, you must first be a servant to God, have a close relationship with Him, and serve Him out of deep loyalty, love, and respect. We are called to walk in Jesus' footsteps, laying down our lives for lost souls so they will know Him. Our attitudes should be the same as that of Christ Jesus.

> Who, being in very nature God, did not consider equality with God something to be grasped, but made Himself nothing, taking the very nature of a servant, being make in human likeness. And being found in appearance as a man, He humbled Himself and became obedient to death, even death on a cross. (Philippians 2:6-8 NIV)

Service implies humility and obedience. True power and greatness come through giving ourselves to others to honor Christ.

> Whoever serves me must follow me; and where I am, my servant also will be. My Father will honor the one who serves me. (John 12:26 NIV)

> The reverent and worshipful fear of the Lord is the beginning [chief and choice part] of Wisdom, and the knowledge of the Holy One is insight and understanding. For by me [wisdom from God] your days shall be

multiplied, and the years of your life she be increased."
(Proverbs 9:10-11 AB)

If we fear God, we will serve Him; if we fear man, we will serve man. There are blessings when we fear God and serve Him. God wants us to serve Him out of desire rather than compulsion, so true believers will serve Him because they want to, not because they are afraid of the flames of hell or because they are forced into service.

Jesus manifested God's glory wherever He went. Every time He entered a situation, things changed; everyone and everything either came into divine order or fled, as did the demons. When God's manifested presence is in the church, all things come in divine order.

God desires intimacy with His people; he wants us to know who He is and what He is doing. God came to dwell in us; it was never His intention to merely visit with us. He is not looking for a place to visit; He is looking for a place to stay.

God wants to share with us His desires, secrets, and wisdom that have been hidden from creation for ages. Revelation will lead us to God, but that revelation is progressive. Without progressive revelation, we cannot move forward in God's purpose. Our carnal insight and divine revelation are different.

Let us not fall into the trap of camping around a doctrine or past movements. Let us move on to the full display of His presence. There is a price to pay, however; we will have to come to places in our lives where we will say there is nothing worth living for other than fulfilling God's will.

Many Christians say, "I have fought the good fight of faith and finished the course" long before they should. They have decided they have suffered long enough and paid enough of a price. Those who have this mind-set will never go into the deep, vast, and limitless purpose of God for their lives. We have just begun; there is so much more of God to experience.

If you are willing, God will take you into His presence and allow you to experience dimensions of intimacy and fellowship beyond your imagination. The fullness of sonship awaits you. Are you willing to pay the price? Ask yourself how much of God do you want to experience and what price you are willing to pay. Are you willing to give up everything as Jesus did and become a slave, or do you want to hold onto your life?

Remember, the law is summed up in a single command: Love your neighbor as yourself. Serve one another in love and you will fulfill the command of Jesus.

Pray with me: Father, I thank you for loving me enough to send your Son to die for my sins. I have no life apart from Him. I surrender my all to you for whatever purpose you desire. I rid myself of all preconceived ideas and notions about who you are, and I say, "Teach me your ways and give me an undivided heart that I may please you." I forsake all for you, my Lord and Savior, God and King. Do with me what you will; I avail myself to you.

# In Closing

While I was praying on September 26, 2007, the Lord gave me this word: "Beware of the Spirit of Deception."

> Now, dear brothers and sisters, let us clarify some things about the coming of our Lord Jesus Christ and how we will be gathered to meet him. Don't be so easily shaken or alarmed by those who say that the day of the Lord has already begun. Don't believe them, even if they claim to have had a spiritual vision, a revelation, or a letter supposedly from us. Don't be fooled by what they say.

> For that day will not come until there is a great rebellion against God and the man of lawlessness is revealed—the one who brings destruction. He will exalt himself and defy everything that people call god and every object of worship. He will even sit in the temple of God, claiming that he himself is God. Don't you remember that I told you about all this when I was with you? And you know what is holding him back, for he can be revealed only when his time comes.

> For this lawlessness is already at work secretly, and it will remain secret until the one who is holding it back steps out of the way. Then the man of lawlessness will

be revealed, but the Lord Jesus will kill him with the breath of his mouth and destroy him by the splendor of his coming. This man will come to do the work of Satan with counterfeit power and signs and miracles.

He will use every kind of evil deception to fool those on their way to destruction, because they refuse to love and accept the truth that would save them. So God will cause them to be greatly deceived, and they will believe these lies. Then they will be condemned for enjoying evil rather than believing the truth. (2 Thessalonians 2:1-12)

Many men and women of God are falling into sin because of the spirit of deception and are seduced by the sweetness of temptation. Their sin has been hidden so long that they don't believe God will expose it. They have fed the body of Christ a watered-down version of the gospel because of their sin. Though the Lord has given them space to repent, they have not taken heed. They are still looking for a way of escape, and the Lord is showing them He is the only way. They must repent, pray, seek the Lord, and get back in the ark of safety, His Word.

The body of Christ must return to the Father's house, where it can be stripped down to nothing so He can be revealed. This is not the time to play church; the body of Christ must become the church. Hidden sin is about to be exposed. God is holy, and He will have a holy people. Submit yourselves to God and resist the Devil, who will flee you. God has prepared a place for you in His presence where no harm can befall you. Bring yourselves before the Lord. Repent, repent, repent, and allow God to cleanse you. Fervently seek His face while He may be found.

There are those who understand the times (Issachar one of the sons of Jacob by Leah who understood the times), who have fortified themselves with the Word and prayer. These men and women are humble, compassionate, careful, deliberate, and not easily excited or disturbed when in high places. They have strength of character and work until they fall asleep. They are strong spiritually and as carriers of the cross. These Issachars see through the eyes of the Spirit, so they plan and prepare for what's coming. Prepare—don't be taken by surprise. "Watch and pray so that you will not fall into temptation. The spirit is willing, but the flesh is weak" (Matthew 26:41 NIV).

God is calling the body of Christ to a position of accountability and responsibility. As believers, we are spiritually blessed. God has imparted revelation truth to us through His Word and through His servants throughout the ages. He has elevated us to positions of sons of God, so we are accountable to Him for what we do with the revelation knowledge, talents, time, finances, resources, and all else He has given us. "For unto whomsoever much is given, of him shall much be required" (Luke 12:48 NIV).

Not only will we be accountable to God on the day of judgment; God is bringing us to a position of accountability now. Consider this prayerfully and ask yourself:

- What am I doing with the revelation knowledge God has given me?
- Have I been faithful with all that God has placed in my hands?
- Am I devoting my time, energy, talents, and finances to winning souls for the kingdom of God?
- Am I living my life according to the revelation I have received?
- Am I busy fulfilling the will of God?

These are the last of the last days. Before we can take our position as God's people of destiny, we must be willing to become accountable to God, accept our responsibility, and discipline our lives so they line up with the Word of God. I urge and entreat you to seek the Lord with your whole heart, become intimate with Him, and experience joy unspeakable when He calls you "friend."

# SELECT BIBLIOGRAPHY

Gee, Donald. *The Fruit of the Spirit*. Springfield, MO: Gospel Publishing House, 1995.

Getz, Gene. *Serving One Another: How Do You Measure Up as a Christian Servant?* Wheaton, IL: Victor Books, 1995.

Hagin, Kenneth, Sr. *Why Tongues*. Winston-Salem, NC: Hagin Ministries, 1975.

Kenyon, E. W. *The Two Kinds of Faith: Faith's Secret Revealed*. Lynwood, WA: Kenyon's Gospel Publishing Society, 1942/1998.

Lake, John G. *Your Power in the Holy Spirit*. New Kensington, PA: Whitaker House, 2010.

Munroe, Myles. *Understanding the Purpose and Power of Prayer*. New Kensington, PA: Whitaker House, 2002.

Nee, Watchman. *Spiritual Authority*. New York, NY: Christian Fellowship Publishers, 1972.

Price, Frederick K. C. *How Faith Works* (revised and expanded). Los Angeles, CA: Faith One Publishing, 2001.

Thieme, R. B., Jr. *The Faith-Rest Life*. Houston, TX: R. B. Thieme, Jr. Bible Ministries, 1961.